Grantland Rice
and His Heroes

Grantland Rice and His Heroes

THE SPORTSWRITER
AS MYTHMAKER
IN THE 1920S

Mark Inabinett

The University of Tennessee Press • Knoxville

Copyright © 1994 by The University of Tennessee Press / Knoxville.
All Rights Reserved. Manufactured in the United States of America.
First Edition.

The paper in this book meets the minimum requirements of the
American National Standard for Permanence of Paper for Printed
Library Materials. ∞   The binding materials have been chosen
for strength and durability.

Library of Congress Cataloging-in-Publication Data

Inabinett, Mark.
    Grantland Rice and his heroes: the sportswriter as mythmaker in the 1920s / Mark
Inabinett. — 1st ed.
        p.   cm.
    Includes bibliographical references (p.   ) and index.
    ISBN 0–87049–848–7 (cloth: alk. paper) — ISBN 0–87049–849–5 (pbk.: alk. paper)
    1. Rice, Grantland, 1800–1954. 2. Sportswriters—United States—Case studies.
3. Sports journalism—United States—Case studies. I. Title.
GV742.42.R53I53   1994   94–6088
070.4'49796—dc20   CIP

Frontispiece: Grantland Rice shows off his golf swing, which, by all accounts, was a good
one. Courtesy, Vanderbilt University Photographic Archives.
Photographs courtesy of UPI/Bettmann Newsphotos: pages 27, 39, 76, and 89.
Photographs courtesy of The Bettmann Archive: pages 52, and 65.

Contents

Illustrations

For they've finished up their hiking through the endless rains of France,
They have made their final sortie and have known their last advance,
They have known their share of horror where the steel was red and wet,
And they'd like to play forever where a fellow might forget.

—Grantland Rice,
"The Return to Sport," 1919

Grantland Rice was making immortals of the Ruths, the Cobbs and the Speakers, as he had done with the great Mathewson.

—Allison Danzig and Peter Brandwein,
Sport's Golden Age, 1969

Beginnings

I came across Grantland Rice's name often in my schoolwork as a child. Usually these encounters came in the form of "in the words of Grantland Rice" or "as Grantland Rice wrote," followed by a glowing description of Ruth, Cobb, Speaker, Mathewson, or some other athlete who had played decades before I was born.

I spent a great deal of my primary education studying sports. My classmates labored over reading, writing, and arithmetic; I reveled in baseball, basketball, and football. I wheedled sports into every class and subject; my permanent report topic in social studies was "sports in whatever country we're studying this semester." Once, after giving my umpteenth book report on a sports biography, the teacher, either in exasperation or admiration of my single-mindedness, said, "Mark, if you don't grow up to be a ballplayer or a sportswriter or a TV sports announcer, then you have truly missed your calling."

In my childhood reading, I repeatedly came across references to the Golden Age of Sports. The writers of my books called on Rice to add his testimony to their descriptions of the era's athletic magnificence. During this Golden Age, every sport had an invincible champion who performed feats both courageous and outrageous with astounding regularity. I, already a connoisseur of sports greatness, had been born at the wrong time; I should have been my grandfather.

As a southerner, I was well aware of the romantic allure of the past. But the practicality of my ongoing Methodist upbringing checked the impulse to long for these reputed halcyon days. Upon reflection, it appeared no more probable to me that every sport's ultimate champion would arise in the span of a single decade than that all my mother's front-yard flowers would bloom at the same instant. My grandfather, looking away from the "NBC Game of the Week," would say, "With a man on third and less than two out, I'd take Ty Cobb over anybody. He'd get that run home." I knew all about Cobb; he'd been the subject of several of my book reports. My grandfather could argue Cobb's merits until he was blue in the face. I'd take Carl Yastrzemski. Had Cobb, or any other player, ever won a pennant practically by himself the way Yaz did for the Red Sox in 1967? Did any of these Golden Age wonders have the grit and savvy Yaz showed whenever the Bosox played on television? For that matter, how could anyone say with assurance that athletes four decades removed were better than the sports stars of my present? How could Bobby Jones, even with his grand slam, stand up against a charge by Arnold Palmer, a shock of hair falling charismatically across his forehead as he whipped the golf ball off the tee? And don't tell me Big Bill Tilden playing in long pants could beat Rocket Rod Laver in tennis. Couldn't Muhammad Ali float like a butterfly and sting like a bee against Jack Dempsey? Vince Lombardi must have inspired the Green Bay Packers as effectively as Knute Rockne ever did the Notre Dame football team.

I had seen the top athletes of my time succeed and, sometimes, fail on television. For the Golden Age heroes, I had only the books to go on, the words of historians and writers. They made a powerful case. The great running back of my day had been tagged the Juice, and he was followed by Sweetness. The image those nicknames conjured on the playing field of the mind paled against that evoked by the Galloping Ghost from the Golden Age.

What, then, made the Golden Age golden? Is the period remembered this way because the athletes of the time possessed unapproachable skill? Or has its glow endured because of the words used to record their achievements? Could it be that the Golden Age was the product of skillful gilding by that era's sportswriters? I think the answers to those questions can be found with the help of Grantland Rice.

Rice seemed to connect the Golden Age athletic stars, like the chain on a necklace of flawless pearls. As the leading sportswriter of the day, Rice wrote often about the athletes who supposedly made the age golden. He is celebrated as the pioneer and leading practitioner of a writing style employing hyperbole and lyricism to convey vivid images. Even his attitude seems to fit the mold of a legend maker, for he said, "When a sportswriter stops making heroes out of athletes, it's time to get out of the business."[1] These factors make Rice central to the examination of the role of the sportswriter in establishing the images of the athletic heroes of the Golden Age. By looking at Rice's work, one might see a connection between Rice's words and the larger-than-life images enjoyed by the sports stars, if such a connection exists.

Such a connection is at least assumed by some. But previous studies of this subject seem to me to have missed the mark, precisely because they did not focus on Rice. In his 1972 master's thesis "Sports Journalism in the 1920s: A Study of the Interdependence of the Daily Newspaper and the Sports Hero," Robert Kilborn, Jr., of Michigan State University concluded sportswriters helped create the Golden Age legends by taking the concept of heroism in sports seriously, refusing to tamper with established heroic images, and declining to get close enough to the heroes to see their flaws.[2] In his book *Sports World: An American Dreamland*, Robert Lipsyte concluded the Golden Age legends were "tunes composed on portable typewriters by gifted, ambitious, often cynical men."[3]

Yet Rice, acknowledged as the most influential sportswriter of the Golden Age, spent countless hours with the sports stars of the day and knew them intimately. And cynicism hardly seems the trait of a man who privately admitted to feeling a great sense of satisfaction when players he selected for his annual All-America football team in *Collier's* went on to success in nonathletic endeavors.[4]

The Golden Age seemed long ago and far away when I read about it as a child. This perception came not only from the obvious, that the age ended nearly thirty years before my birth, but also from more subtle reasons. The athletes seemed to have characteristics more suitable for shining knights of Camelot than for sports stars, especially because my own hero, Yaz, often held out in spring training for a more lucrative contract. The sports world seemed different, too; smaller, certainly, with basketball and professional football given about as much notice as soccer is today. When the Golden Age began at the end of World War I, major-league baseball and college football were the major sports of interest. Boxing quickly gained a new respectability after the war, and the leading events in golf and tennis surged into national interest as part of the sports boom. In fact, events in two of these new major sports can serve as boundaries for the Golden Age. The Jack Dempsey–Jess Willard heavyweight championship fight on July 4, 1919, was the first big-time sports event after the war's end. Eleven years later, with the Great Depression ready to crush the nation into weary poverty, Bobby Jones became the only player to complete the grand slam of golf by winning the U.S. Amateur championship for his fourth major title of 1930.

In the study of the relationship between Rice's work and the public's perception of the Golden Age heroes, I have renewed acquaintance with some of my boyhood friends, books collected at Christmas and on birthdays from a perceptive family. But other books have proven more helpful on the specific topic dealt with here, particularly anthologies that include Rice's works from the 1920s, such as *The Best of Grantland Rice* and *Wake Up the Echoes: From the Sports Pages of the New York Herald-Tribune*. In addition to the works found here, I also have examined a large selection of Rice's stories and columns as they appeared in the *New York*

Tribune and the *New York Herald-Tribune* in the 1920s, and Rice's weekly articles in *Collier's* from 1924 to 1931. The best book of background on the period is *Sport's Golden Age: A Close-Up of the Fabulous Twenties*, which was written by the sportswriters of the era and includes a revealing introduction by Rice. The best book about the sportswriters of the period is Jerome Holtzman's fascinating volume of interviews with sports reporters, *No Cheering in the Press Box*.

Those writings are full of the exploits of the Golden Age giants. But even among giants, six figures tower above the rest in their deeds and, to an even greater degree, in the popular mind of America. Jack Dempsey, Babe Ruth, Bobby Jones, Bill Tilden, Red Grange, Knute Rockne—names consigned by the years not to trivia but to enduring places in our culture.

Their images, what Rice wrote about them, and how he affected them will be examined in chapters devoted to each of these men. But first, we need to meet their time and their maker.

CHAPTER 1

Grantland Rice

When Grantland Rice joined *Collier's* as a weekly contributor in 1924, the magazine carried an announcement that read, "To a multitude of readers his name spells color, dash, action, drama—as well as honesty and soundness."[1] The magazine's management was proud of its new association with the most famous and influential sportswriter of the day. In the seventy years since this announcement, however, the way in which Rice imparted that color, dash, action, and drama has come to be written off as quaint, indicative of a more innocent age. The seemingly sophisticated modern sportswriters who know of Rice at all often view his style as being as archaic and embarrassingly naïve as the old practice of bloodletting. This perception is narrow and unfair.

Rice saw heroes in athletes. Much as Rice's view of these athletes was only a slice of all they were, so the surviving image of Rice's work is one-dimensional. The reigning perception of Rice has been built around a few pieces of work, judged by present-day standards rather than by those under which he wrote. In the sixty or so years since Rice wrote his most memorable pieces, a parade of apologists has made excuses for him, apparently embarrassed by his writing when looking back from a post–Golden Age vantage point. This group has forgotten what sportswriter Red Smith said of Rice: "Make no mistake about Granny: he was a giant. Some of his stuff seems like immature gushing today, but he was exactly right for his time, and if he had lived in another time he would have been right for that one."[2]

Rice has been characterized as a perpetually sunny cheer-leader, hyperbolic praiser, and moralizing sentimentalist. At times he was. His enduring reputation as such rests on fragments of two works—the lead to his report on the 1924 Notre Dame–Army football game and the last two lines of the poem "Alumnus Foot-ball." *Bartlett's Familiar Quotations* includes both.

The football lead transformed Notre Dame's backs into Fam-ine, Pestilence, Destruction, and Death—the Four Horsemen of the Apocalypse. The lead garnered so much attention that it firmly established the era of metaphor and hyperbole in sports report-ing. Later writers sarcastically speculated that Rice must have lain on the field in order to see the Horsemen "outlined against a blue-gray October sky," as the opening line states.[3]

Rice ended "Alumnus Football" with the lines:

> For when the One Great Scorer comes to mark against your name,
> He writes—not that you won or lost—but how you played the
> Game.[4]

The selections reflect Rice's style and outlook accurately, but not completely. Stanley Woodward, former sports editor of the *New York Herald-Tribune,* wrote that Rice became sportswriting's most successful syndicated columnist "more through his never-failing craftsmanship and punctuality than through occasional flights of lilting poetry and apt characterizations, such as the Four Horsemen."[5]

Without a doubt, Rice believed his lines from "Alumnus Foot-ball" to be true. He wrote in *Collier's* in 1925: "The main idea back of sport should be recreation in pursuit of health and pleasure: competitions that help to build up clean living, cool heads, stout hearts and sound judgment under fire. Victory is, of course, the more pleasing destiny, but it isn't the entire destiny."[6]

By his nature, Rice would seem a writer more inclined to praise than vilify. Former sportswriter Paul Gallico has written of Rice's work: "The personality of Grantland Rice shone through his columns—that of a sweet, gentle man with something endearingly childlike about him, who passionately loved his work and his world."[7] Rice wrote of his reporting style: "I've had no particular philosophy in covering sports. I've just reported what I've seen. If anything, I give the other guy a break. That's because I've been an athlete and made mistakes, too. In a 2-0 baseball game, for instance, I tend to give the pitcher credit for pitching a good game, instead of belaboring the other team for poor hitting."[8]

The memoirs of sportswriters who worked with him portray Rice as a man who lived the lines he wrote in "Alumnus Football." In 1944 Stanley Frank wrote of Rice, "Everyone loves the guy. There is hardly a sportswriter alive who has not been the beneficiary of Rice's experience and friendship."[9]

Rice often alluded to higher powers in describing the exploits of sports stars, a tactic some of his colleagues used when describing him. Henry McLemore called Rice "an angel with a *Racing Form* tucked under one wing,"[10] and Red Smith wrote, "I think Granny was a saint who swore and drank and bet on horses, the kind of saint a person would love to be around."[11] Smith also wrote that Rice stood for sportsmanship, honesty, kindness, courtesy, integrity, and faith.[12] Rice took on the heroic proportion he imparted to his athletic idols. Marshall Hunt, a former New York baseball writer, has raised perhaps the only discouraging words concerning Rice in any retrospective view. Hunt complained to Jerome Holtzman when Holtzman was gathering material for his book *No Cheering in the Press Box:* "There were many controversial issues of our times, stories that were hot and full of meat. But Grant never got involved. He never bit into anything. I used to tell other writers that I didn't like his stuff, that it was all floss. And a few of them would say, 'Oh, why the idea of you criticizing Grantland Rice.'"[13]

Rice had no illusions about how he worked and the attitude behind his approach. He wrote, "No one has ever accused your humble but cheerful correspondent of being a calamity howler.

He has always preferred looking on the sunny side of things; and he hasn't spent much time peering into the shadows searching for ghosts of trouble and phantoms of sorrow."[14]

If Rice were nothing more than a showy stylist whose work always skimmed the surface of sports' bright side, he could be dismissed as merely an evangelist of fun. Although his personality demanded he have a positive style, the virtues he condoned would not allow Rice to ignore the negative aspects of athletics in his times. Because of his preference for the virtuous and valiant in sports, Rice often wrote about the corrupting influence of greed on games. In 1927, he used a column to run his poem "Modern Sport," which began:

> Money to the left of them and money to the right,
> Money everywhere they turn from morning through the night;
> Only two things count at all from mountain to the sea,
> Part of it's percentage, and the rest is guarantee.[15]

Although he denied newspapers had created the surge in sports interest in the 1920s, Rice understood the connection between media exposure and athletic reputation. He wrote in a 1927 column:

> Professional football has shown one thing about college football. In college football, certain stars . . . nearer centers of publicity are lifted to fame.
>
> They are handed the laurel in large chunks. Some of them take up pro football. And as often as not these stars in pro football are badly outplayed by entries from smaller colleges and universities barely heard of before. If some of these unknown stars were on bigger university teams, the ones that draw most of the public notice, they would be rated well above many others who draw the higher rating.[16]

When Rice did criticize, he could do so with the same hyperbole he used to glorify, as during the 1926 World Series, when he called

Yankee shortstop Mark Koenig "the ill-fated son of destiny who must have killed an albatross in his youth to become an ancient mariner of woe," or as when describing a muffed double play in a report from a World Series game between the Yankees and the Reds: "It was here that the unkempt fates planted the crown of thorns upon the unlucky brow of Bill Myers, the Red shortstop. Bill Dickey rapped one to Lonnie Frey at second for the easiest, the simplest and surest double play in World Series history. It was the type of double play that could have been handled by an infield combination from an orphan asylum with cramp colic."[17]

Four factors have enabled Rice's work to influence the image of sports in the 1920s: the perceived authenticity of his stories, the weight history has given his judgments, the suitability of his style for his audience, and his exposure and fame.

Rice might have known more top sports figures than any other sportswriter in history. He spent many hours in the company of the sports heroes of the 1920s, whether it was hosting a Saturday evening open house during the college football season for coaches in the New York City area, drinking "Tennessee milk" in his apartment with Knute Rockne, watching Babe Ruth shoot off doorknobs with a rifle, or going to Coney Island with Bobby Jones. Modern reporters might say Rice endangered his objectivity by losing his journalistic distance. But the time he spent with the sports stars and the intimate knowledge he gained of their characters and backgrounds translated into columns that gave readers a look at the heroes that no other reporter provided. When Paul Gallico left sports writing in 1936, he wrote:

> The sportswriter has few if any heroes. We create many because it is our business to do so, but we do not believe in them. We know them too well. We are concerned as often, sometimes, with keeping them and their weaknesses and peccadillos out of the paper as we are with putting them in. . . . We sing of their muscles, their courage, their gameness and their skill because it seems to amuse readers and sells papers, but we rarely consider them as people

and strictly speaking, leave their characters alone because that is
dangerous ground.[18]

It was precisely this willingness to travel such dangerous ground
that set Rice apart from his colleagues. He did write about character, and in doing so, he humanized the athletic supermen. At
the same time, he was not interested particularly in exposing
weaknesses and peccadilloes, and this allowed his many contacts
to relax and talk openly in his company. Rice wrote of his relationship with his sources: "I've gotten almost as many columns
while playing a round of golf with this or that person as I've
gleaned from the press box. . . . I've got a host of columns from
the locker room . . . not only about and with name golfers but
about and with headliners of every sport and business. Peeled
down to his shorts, a highball in one hand, an attested score card
in the other, it's hard for a man to be anything but himself."[19]

If, as Gallico asserts, Rice's contemporaries did not believe in
their own athletic heroes, perhaps that explains in part why the best
writers moved on to other endeavors while Rice alone stayed in
sports. He was a true believer. In the foreword to his autobiography, Rice wrote:

> Almost every one of these heroes of sport taught me something,
> gave me some insight into how to live and added to my philoso-
> phy of life. And, I think these champions and the way that they
> lived have something to say to all of us. . . . To reach the top in
> any sport—or in life—you need confidence and belief in yourself.
> Can you imagine Babe Ruth ever considering the possibility of
> failure? Many years ago, Babe told me, "Once my swing starts, I
> can't change it or pull up. It's all or nothing at all."[20]

For all of his hyperbole, Rice wrote with honesty. He believed in
his heroes, not because of naïveté but because he knew them. He
often imparted this knowledge in a style his readers found dy-
namic. His strong imagery allowed readers to see what he had

seen. Rice genuinely loved sports, and he also understood the elements of a good story. He wrote in 1924:

> My life as a follower of sport has been one thrill after another: big thrills and little thrills—thrills of all descriptions marching by with the seasons, and always I have the knowledge that there are new and possibly greater thrills to come.
>
> There has been the thrill of the new star suddenly coming to fame on some great play, and the deeper thrill of the fading veteran coming back for another whack at glory after he was supposed to have been down and out. The basis of the big thrill in sport is the uprising against heavy odds, the smaller man beating the larger one, the has-been coming back, the battered and broken rising to heights of glory.[21]

Rice's kinship with his readers and closeness to his subjects gave his work a ring of authenticity, as did his long experience as a sports observer. When Rice assessed Jack Dempsey's chances of retaining the heavyweight championship after three years of inactivity, he based his outlook on his knowledge of the sport. A similar layoff had preceded each of the losses by the previous heavyweight titleholders. Rice did not relate this information with the dusty air of a historian checking records, but as someone who had seen in the ring the seven previous champions, as someone who had witnessed the great fights of the past and remembered.[22]

Rice began syndication of his column "The Sportlight" in 1913. Before the 1920s ended, he had become the first nationally famous sportswriter in the United States, with his column appearing in more than 250 papers. During the 1920s, Rice became involved with every means of sports coverage, and his income rose past $100,000 per year. In addition to his syndicated column and weekly piece for *Collier's*, Rice reported for the *New York Herald-Tribune*, contributed free-lance material to magazines, edited *American Golfer* magazine, and supervised Sportlight Films, which

produced once-a-month, ten-minute newsreels devoted to athletics.[23] Rice also handled the first World Series radio broadcast
from a ball park in 1922. An estimated one million people in a
three-hundred-mile area around New York heard Rice's description of the World Series that year.[24] Rice even wrote the script
for the first movie to star a baseball player: *Somewhere in Georgia,*
with Ty Cobb in the lead as a baseball-playing bank clerk kid-
napped on the eve of the big game.[25] Rice accomplished this while
traveling about fifteen thousand miles a year.

Rice's views on sports reached more readers than anyone
else's. When he captured a feeling in a phrase, such as with his
Galloping Ghost nickname for Red Grange, the phrase went nationwide. Red Smith believed that Rice did as much for football
through his writing as any man who ever lived.[26] The nicknames
Rice hung on his heroes have stuck with them since. Rice used
the nickname Praying Colonels, which coach Charley Morgan
had devised for his team at tiny Centre College in Kentucky when
he led it on a brief rampage through big-time football. Morgan
played up the prayer meeting the team held before each kickoff
to garner publicity for his unheralded squad. Once, as the team
checked into a New York City hotel, Morgan saw Rice entering
the lobby. He immediately turned to his supposedly pious players and barked, "Down on your knees, quick, you bastards; here
comes Grantland Rice."[27]

Rice influenced not only readers across the United States but
also sportswriters. In Rice's obituary, Arthur Daley, the *New York
Times*'s Pulitzer Prize–winning sports columnist, wrote: "It's to
be doubted that any man had a more profound effect on the
sportswriting profession than our beloved dean. He gave it fire
and enthusiasm and sparkle. . . . He could reflect the drama and
the excitement as few men could. There was an era in the 1920s
when every young writer tried to emulate Grantland Rice."[28]

Unlike most of his predecessors, Rice brought a solid educa-
tional background to sports writing. He was a Phi Beta Kappa
graduate of Vanderbilt, where he played baseball and football

and majored in Greek and Latin. Although primarily a sports-writer to the day he died in 1954, while typing his syndicated column, he had done more than write sports. In his first job (for five dollars a week) with the *Nashville News* in his hometown in 1901, he covered the state capitol and the county courthouse and handled general assignments in addition to his sports duties. After working with the *Atlanta Constitution* and *Cleveland News*, he returned to Nashville to work with the *Tennessean*, where he also wrote a daily column of verse and covered the theater beat.[29] When he traveled, which was almost all the time, he carried two suitcases—one for clothes and one for books.[30]

His best work, loaded with the imagery necessary to allow a blind audience to see, seemed decades ahead of the literary journalists who came along in the 1960s. Rice's beginning of a story about the Paris Olympics:

> It was an afternoon of blazing heat, heat blown northward from the Sahara in the wake of a sirocco, heat that was heat. The thermometer was at a hundred or more, and into the blast of this furnace the greatest runners of 30 nations were setting out upon a 10,000-meter cross country whirl. An almost endless parade started. Only a few finished. Along the route there were fine runners unconscious, completely out, with faces upturned to the sun as ambulances came by to rush them along to waiting trainers and physicians. There were others who were reeling and floundering—running a few yards, falling and then rising again as they fought their way. There was courage enough here to make up a war.[31]

Yet Rice also wrote leads that make modern sports editors cringe, such as this one from a World Series game between the Philadelphia Athletics and the St. Louis Cardinals: "Bill Hallahan again shut out the famous maulers from the mansion of Mack with only three scattered blows as the battle ended, 2 to 0."[32]

Few deny Rice's influence on sports reporting. The argument about his influence has come down to the question, Did Rice advance or sidetrack sports journalism? Rice's style unquestionably opened up sports writing. His creative approach extended the entertainment from the field to the page and allowed sports journalists to be both reporters and writers.[33] Stanley Woodward has credited Rice, along with Golden Age contemporaries Westbrook Pegler and W. O. McGeehan, with shaping the modern style of sports reporting: "Rice contributed rhythm and euphony, Pegler a grumping and grudging curiosity for fact, and McGeehan a certain twist which could make an ordinary sentence interesting."[34]

Because many sportswriters who lacked his talent and sensitivity imitated his style, Rice has been blamed for an era of excess in sports reporting. But this seems like blaming Sir Edmund Hilary for the deaths of those who died trying to climb Everest after his own conquest. Stanley Walker, the outstanding city editor of the *New York Herald-Tribune*, held the view that Rice was one of a kind and that most of the imitators were ill equipped to perform at his level: "Grantland Rice, perhaps the most popular and respected gentleman ever to write sports, came out of the South long before the war bearing an unusual equipment—he had a good education, he was a poet at heart, and he had a genuine, almost fanatical, love for sport. . . . He set an example for many a young man, who, seeking to be a word-painter, loaded his popgun with red paint and fired at the rainbow. . . . A school of Rice imitators, never as good as Rice at his best, and much worse than Rice at his worst, grew up."[35]

Shirley Povich, a longtime sportswriter for the *Washington Post*, disagrees with Walker's conventional view. He thinks not Rice, but other reporters, were responsible for spawning the cliché-ridden, overly dramatic style of writing that has given sports reporting a black eye:

> Too many young sportswriters in my era had the wrong writing heroes. Certainly we all admired Runyon and Rice and Pegler, idolized them, but we gave up too quickly and said, "We can never write

like they can." We made the mistake of imitating other, closer heroes—the Associated Press writers, Alan Gould and Jack Bell. Their
copy was regarded as lively copy, and many of us, in our sheer stu-
pidity, assumed, that since they were the stars of the Associated
Press, they had to be fine writers, fine reporters. And we followed
blindly. But those wire service guys were guilty as hell. They were
always writing leads such as "Gene Sarazen and his blazing putter,"
and "Notre Dame came roaring from behind." Every pitcher had
somebody "eating out of the palm of his hand"—all those horrid
metaphors. They made everything cataclysmal. They couldn't give
you a short action word. They were overmoderated, the adjectives
were endless and the same . . . When I see it now, I want to upchuck.[36]

That Rice's writing style lay beyond the reach of others of his day
seems supported by a half-page promotional advertisement run by
the *New York Herald-Tribune,* his home paper at the time, on September 23, 1927, the day of the second Gene Tunney–Jack Dempsey
heavyweight championship fight. Although clearly stilted in the
language of publicity, the ad provides evidence that at the time
Rice's reporting style was recognized and admired for its quality and uniqueness (and also reminds us that money meant everything in the Roaring Twenties):

The eye of a camera, the news sense of a great reporter, the imagination of a poet—that's Grantland Rice. Let Irvin S. Cobb say it: "Rice is
the only man I know who has made literature of the sporting department of a daily paper—matter that has good diction, sharp,
crackling metaphor, deft phrasing, smooth clarified English." Go
with Rice to the big sports events. Read his crisp comment in "The
Sportlight"—with a dash of verse now and then. Enjoy his "Tales
of a Wayside Tee." He is one of the highest paid sports writers in
the world, and he's only one of the brilliant features—plus complete covering of the news of your town and the rest of the world—
that are drawing so many readers to the *Herald Tribune.*[37]

However much Rice's colleagues might have admired or strained to copy his style, they could not duplicate his impact. Rice's national audience and his reputation gave him a unique opportunity in the pre-electronic age to influence public perception of the national sports scene. Rice's access to the top athletic figures of the day allowed him to write often and comprehensively about them. The proficiency with which Rice imprinted his views upon the nation can be seen by comparing Rice's written image of his athletic heroes with the image some of those men have enjoyed in the public mind ever since the Golden Age of Sports.

CHAPTER 2

The Golden Age

In 1925, the *New York Sun* sent Laurence Stallings to Philadelphia to write a feature story on Red Grange's only collegiate football performance outside the Midwest. Stallings's account would accompany the newspaper's game story on the Illinois-Pennsylvania contest. Stallings had written the hard-boiled best seller *What Price Glory?* He had launched a successful career as a playwright after surviving a serious wound and the horrors of trench warfare in Europe during World War I. He didn't normally write sports stories, but in the newspaper terminology of the time, on this occasion he became the *Sun*'s "trained seal."

Grange had a terrific game on an extraordinarily muddy field, gaining 363 yards and scoring three touchdowns. When the contest ended, the sportswriters in the press box set to work, banging out stories on portable typewriters and dictating to telegraph men. Everyone went to work, that is, everyone except Stallings. He began to pace, then to moan in despair. Finally, one of his colleagues asked what was wrong. Stallings cried, "I can't write it! The story's too big for me!"[1]

Not so for the sportswriters. Ever since Grantland Rice had transformed the Notre Dame backfield into the Four Horsemen of the Apocalypse with a single lead, the sports press had regularly used metaphor and hyperbole to create larger-than-life spectacles. The awestruck Stallings had experienced football while under the influence of the sportswriters' imagery. He had not seen Red Grange; he had seen the Galloping Ghost.

In the 1920s, unrivaled heroes seemed to arise on every playing field. It was an era of excess showered with superlatives. The press did not, could not, wait for the perspective of history. It recognized its good fortune, and even before the decade ended, sportswriters referred to the period as the Golden Age. Sportswriters declared that they witnessed a time when the best and brightest flamed across the sports heavens. The stars became so brilliant that the nation turned its gaze to previously closeted sports such as golf and tennis.[2]

From the myopia of 1931, sportswriter Paul Gallico wrote of the decade just concluded: "Never before had there been a period when, from the ranks of every sport, arose some glamorous, unbeatable figure who shattered record after record, spread-eagled his field and drew into the box office an apparently unending stream of gold and silver. We have lived through a decade of deathless heroes."[3]

Babe Ruth stuffed himself with hot dogs and stayed out all night and still hit home runs farther and more frequently than anyone had before. Jack Dempsey carried so much power in his fists he lifted boxing from illegality to million-dollar social function. Red Grange became the supernatural Galloping Ghost, beyond the touch of mortal tacklers, and record crowds came to his hauntings. Bobby Jones and Big Bill Tilden straddled golf and tennis as invincible champions. Knute Rockne turned boys into men with his magic half-time orations to his ceaselessly winning Notre Dame football teams. Man o' War became the fastest horse, Johnny Weissmuller the fastest swimmer, Charles Paddock the fastest runner—ever. The newspapers established these things in the celestial firmament of folklore.

The sports pages alone did not have a monopoly on the nation's heroes and celebrities. Charles Lindbergh, a stunt pilot who flew alone across the Atlantic Ocean to win a prize, became the hero of the age. Lucky Lindy, the Flying Fool, set off a spate of solo flights as pilots sought to be the first to fly from any point A to any point B over some intervening body of water. The nation's women did a mass swoon over screen star Rudolph Valentino. Shipwreck Kelly pushed all but the booming business news off the front pages by sitting on a flagpole in Baltimore for twenty-three days.[4]

The United States of the 1920s seemed to hunger for heroes and celebrities. Perhaps the end to the horrors of a world war released a burst of childlike exuberance. Maybe the emergence of the nation as a young and strong world power passed on to the population the confidence to flex its muscles and show off. Maybe the collective consciousness of the war years gave way to a desire to cheer the triumph of the individual. Perhaps the new leisure created by the thriving economy created a void. Or maybe the reason for the sports boom of the 1920s was as simple as the need to play.

Rice was one of the first to foresee the new era of sports that followed the war to end all wars. In an article for the June 1919 issue of *Country Life,* Rice wrote:

> With the return of peace it was only natural that there should be a great rush back to sport again. There was first of all an almost universal desire for recreation and for play. There was also a great desire for the thrills of competition not quite so closely associated with death and devastation, where it was more man against man, rather than man against machine. . . . They had been held in so long as part of a vast machine that each one felt the old desire to frolic again, with his individual freedom no longer restrained. . . . 1920 will bring the greatest international competition that sport and outdoor life have ever known.[5]

The returning servicemen brought with them a new interest in sports. Military training had introduced thousands of men to a diversity of sports, providing the largest stimulus for athletics in the country's history. For example, before the war boxing was a disreputable, outlawed sport. The U.S. Army used boxing to provide a foundation for bayonet fighting, and in 1918, sixty thousand men watched a series of bouts between the U.S. Eighty-sixth Division and Canadian troops. After the war, the American Legion led the movement to repeal bans on boxing.[6]

A nation weary of war greeted its doughboys with revived optimism. The final fight for democracy had been won, and the country turned its attention away from world affairs. The most important leagues became the American and the National, not Woodrow Wilson's group of nations. The first year after the war's end brought changes and uncertainty: the Treaty of Versailles, prohibition, woman's suffrage, race riots, and red scares. Sociologists contend the combination created a need for visible symbols of stability.[7]

Postwar technology helped reduce the work week from sixty to forty-eight hours. The automobile made the nation mobile. Sports events became more accessible, and people had the time and money to attend them. In his book *America as Civilization: Life and Thought in the United States Today*, Max Lerner wrote of the 1920s: "There are few parallels in history to an American culture which was presented overnight with the gift of leisure, not just to one class but to almost the entire culture. Americans have found in sports a set of loyalties that in past cultures have been linked with more destructive pursuits. They have also found in it a kind of substitute for an urban culture's loss of relation to the natural environment."[8]

Although technology freed workers from slavish hours, it hastened the urbanization of the nation into faceless masses. Sports provided an outlet for individual achievement, as well as an outlet to cheer and celebrate the individual and his achievements. In a society becoming increasingly more complicated and bureaucratic, star athletes gained fame and fortune outside the system. Before the war, the nation's heroes had come from business, industry, and science.[9] For Rice, the American ideal survived unspoiled only in sports:

The true democracy in the United States is not to be found among our politicians, our so-called statesmen, our labor union leaders or our capitalists. It is only to be found in sport.

I already have given you the stories of Babe Ruth, Walter Hagen, Billy Burke, Gene Sarazen, Jack Dempsey and others, orphans, caddies or roustabouts, who rose to fame and wealth through their own ability and skill. There is no class distinction, no union or capital protection in sport. Here you are measured by what you are and what you can do. Nothing else counts.[10]

The economy thrived in the 1920s, and promoters and chambers of commerce found profit in capitalizing on the country's obsession with sports. Athletics became more than fun and games; it became big business. The magic words: one million. The 1926 World Series became the first to take in more than one million dollars from attendance. Jack Dempsey drew the first five one-million-dollar gates in boxing history. The Yankees became the first team to attract one million fans in a season.[11]

The 1920s became the Golden Age of Sports for all of these reasons. But the foundation for an athletic utopia would have to be the athletes themselves. According to Rice, "This postwar period gave the game the greatest collection of stars that sport has ever known since the first cave man tackled the mammoth and the aurochs bull."

It seems improbable that every sport's ultimate champion arose in the same ten-year period. Yet the heroes of the Golden Age have endured as if that happened. The appeal of these heroes and legends reached beyond the hard-core sports fan, who had the inside knowledge of the games needed to evaluate their abilities and place in context their achievements. The sports stars became household names as the sportswriters conveyed more than the game to the readers. The personalities of the heroes, projected by the sportswriters, enhanced their appeal. Rice wrote: "Skill and ability were not the major factors in this Golden Age.

It was their color and their crowd appeal, their vivid splash against the skyline, their remembered deeds, that write their story. . . . They had something more than mere skill or competitive ability. They also had in record quality and quantity that indescribable asset known as color, personality, crowd appeal, or whatever you may care to call it."[12]

The sports heroes made good copy. Having portrayed the players as more than mortal in their on-the-field exploits, some of the sportswriters balanced their portraits by emphasizing the humanity of the heroes, their closeness, off the field, to the average man. Rice noted in 1924 an empathy between fans and their heroes: "Life in the main is a battle against odds of one sort or another. The road to the top is always uphill and the onlooker at a sporting event senses in the struggle on the field a repetition of his own struggle in everyday life. . . . He rises or he falls with his hero. It is a part of his own experience."[13]

Reporters told the American fairy tale of real-life Horatio Alger characters over and over. Babe Ruth, who had spent his childhood in St. Mary's Industrial Home for incorrigible boys, eventually earned a salary larger than that of the president.[14] Knute Rockne immigrated from Norway as a five-year-old and became not only the personification of college football but also the head of sales promotion for the Studebaker Corporation.

Reporters no longer confined their attentions to the playing fields, but, in the extra space devoted to sports, analyzed strategy, provided background, and illuminated character. "Unless he grows up to be President or defendant in an important murder trial, the college football player is likely to receive more extensive and searching newspaper publicity in his undergraduate days than at any other period in his life," Heywood Broun wrote of the spotlight the press had turned on football in particular and sports in general.[15] The Associated Press created an eight-man sports department in 1927 and quickly added four more reporters. The volume of sports news carried by the United Press tripled between 1925 and 1928.[16] By 1925, the average metropolitan news-paper carried two thousand inches of sports copy each week, twice the amount devoted to sports in 1915.[17] W. P. Beazell, assistant managing editor of the *New York World,* said of his paper's devotion of 25 percent of its news and forty percent of its local news to sports in the late 1920s, "My intellect is offended, but my editorial judgment approves it."[18] The space reserved for sports in the newspapers expanded to keep pace with the public interest. Some media critics said it was the other way around.

Sportswriter John R. Tunis was one of the most outspoken press critics during the Golden Age. He thought the press had cultivated an artificial interest in sports to boost circulation and that reporters made the overemphasized sports world seem the playground of the valiant and virtuous, all just to capture reader interest. In the *Saturday Evening Post,* Tunis wrote on what he thought was lopsided reporting:

> The American sports lover must not be told that the athletic life of the land is in anything but a healthy condition. To do so would amount to being a traitor to the cause. It would disillusion the newspaper reader; it might quench the inherent idealism in sports which is born and bred in every youngster in the United States. But most of all, it would discourage a potential customer. It would break and not make circulation. Accordingly, the sporting news must be played up as glorious and magnificent; the dull, the shoddy, the secondrate in sports must be left unsaid.[19]

Newspaper circulation increased from 28 million in 1914 to 36 million in 1926, even though the number of daily papers in the United States dropped from 2,580 to 2,001 during that period. A growing literacy rate and increasing economic prosperity made possible the expansion of newspaper circulation.[20] Newspapers took advantage of these factors by devoting more space to sports coverage and thereby capitalizing on the booming interest in athletics and by making the sports pages accessible to all readers. With its roots in the days of yellow journalism, it followed that the sports section would feature slangy and facetious writing. But by the postwar years, the arrival and influence of writers such as Rice had ended the dependence on synthetic jargon and fanciful gibberish that had made most sports writing virtually unintelligible to any but the writers and sports fanatics.[21]

The publicity created by increased newspaper coverage helped popularize and legitimize athletics. Readers had only the sports page to turn to for accounts of Grange or Dempsey. Furthermore, they could verify the reported superhuman abilities only by attending a game or a fight. *Editor and Publisher* reported in 1927: "Present-day opinion of newspaper editors, psychologists, trade-publication editors, advertising men, and journalism instructors is that sports on their present scale would be impossible without the sports section of the daily papers. . . . Without the assistance of the newspapers, sports would never have attained their present popularity. Sports officials are among the first to admit the debt that baseball, football, boxing and other sports owe the papers."[22]

Whether the sports press caused the sports boom or responded to public demand, it certainly shaped the public's perception, because newspapers and magazines provided the country with virtually all its exposure to the sports stars. In a time before television, and before widespread newsreel sports coverage, few fans were able to see the great players. Most people came to know these heroes through the images created by the sportswriters. The sports stories made the heroes larger than life at a time when there were no yardsticks. The treasury of local tales and traditional lore became replenished in the mind of the American boy with baseball's batting averages. And only those who attended games could see first hand the heroes at work and check for themselves the accuracy of the sportswriters' descriptions.[23] George Strickler, former sports editor of the *Chicago Tribune*, wrote of the period:

How many people did Grange play to? Supposing he played to an average of sixty thousand people in those stadiums back in '24. He played nine games a year. That's a half-million a year. He played three years. That a million and a half, and there were a lot of repeaters in those crowds. So you didn't have that many people. Today, with television, a guy comes along and in one afternoon, in one game, sixty-four million people see him. When you see a player, in the flesh or on television, it takes a lot of the romance out of it. . . . The distance lent enchantment.[24]

Sportswriters became poets in the press box, thrill spinners rather than statisticians. With telegraph operators waiting at their elbows to transmit stories as soon as the game ended, the sportswriters wrote rapidly, weaving lush leads, and coining slogans and nicknames that telegraphed images to readers.[25] While Stallings agonized after the Illinois-Pennsylvania football game, Damon Runyon fired back his report to the paper describing Grange as "three or four men and a horse rolled into one."[27]

In the sportwriters' need to create vivid images, their labels became a shorthand. Grange became the Galloping Ghost; Ruth, the Sultan of Swat; Walter Johnson, the Big Train; Dempsey, the Manassa Mauler; and the 1924 Notre Dame backfield, the Four Horsemen of the Apocalypse. Paul Gallico described the work of his colleagues in the 1920s in this way: "Here was not only drama but wit and humor and an expansion of the language. Where ordinary words were inadequate to tell the tale, these men made up their own. They bestowed unforgettable sobriquets on teams and individuals, and coined slogans in use to this very day."[27]

The period produced two discernible schools of sports writing: the Gee-Whiz school, followers of Grantland Rice, and the Aw-Nuts school, disciples of W. O. McGeehan.[28] The Gee-Whiz writers were free with praise and embellishment and seemed satisfied to celebrate and glorify their subjects. Hyperbole and allusions to mythology and history were standard features of their reports. The Aw-Nuts writers were more skeptical and harder to convince of a player's immortality. But when they found a hero who met their standards, the differences between Aw-Nuts and Gee-Whiz became little more than choice of adjective.[29] McGeehan began his 1925 story on the death of Christy Mathewson, "In this sporting game more than in any other walk of life they raise false idols. They make heroes of brutes, they make demigods of inconsequential young men without character or true courage, they make saintly characters out of the vicious." He then proceeded to praise the skills and virtues of Mathewson in a manner worthy of Rice.[30]

Those who have looked at sports writing in the Golden Age from more recent vantage points have snickered at what they perceived as naïveté. In his biography of Ring Lardner, Jonathan Yardley called the predominant style "a bad dream by Sir Walter Scott."[31] Even from a time as close to the Golden Age as 1944, sportswriter Stanley Frank wrote of the style, "By present-day standards, the color is glaring, the straining for effect is self-conscious, the round-eyed wonder is juvenile and a competent copyreader could perform a major operation on the superfluity of words."[32]

The Great Depression brought starkness to the press. In the smaller newspapers of the 1930s, the four-thousand-word sports story with accompanying features and sidebars went the way of the dropkick and mashie niblick. The smaller papers devoted less of their space to sports.[33] Preciseness replaced hyperbole, and the free flow of adjectives tapered to a trickle over sports stars who, not surprisingly, seemed dull and human. Everyone looked back at the glow of the Golden Age and wondered where the heroes had gone. Rice wrote in his autobiography in 1954: "Looking back and reflecting on that golden, crazy age—from 1919 to 1930—I'm convinced, more than ever, that no decade in history has produced the likes of Ruth, Dempsey, Jones, Hitchcock, Man o' War, Weissmuller and Bill Tilden. They had that indefinable but 18-carat touch called 'color,' that put them above the greats of any age."[34]

This may be so. But it was the writers, and chief among them Rice, who recognized the color and burnished it until it shone like a beacon in the minds of the readers. Rice and his colleagues gave the U.S. sports fans the human and the superhuman in their stories, fixing images so firmly in the national consciousness that they have endured for generations in the realm of myth and legend. John Kieran, who began the *New York Times*'s "Sports of the Times" column, wrote of the leading sportswriters of the Golden Age:

> What is sometimes overlooked about that glorious era of competi-
> tion is that there were writers worthy of the great competitors of
> those dazzling days. What would we have known of Achilles,
> Hector, Aeneas, Ulysses, Ajax and other heroes of ancient times if not
> for Homer and Virgil? So the champions of a great era in American
> sports found their personalities and their performances chronicled
> by a great group of writers, men who were outstanding in their
> own part of the field, the press section.[35]

Nearly all of the Golden Age sportswriters who are widely re-membered today achieved their greatest acclaim in other fields. The time in which Ring Lardner, Heywood Broun, Westbrook Pegler, and Damon Runyon displayed their talents on the sports pages has become viewed as a period of training or diversion. Their biographers have written defensively, as if these writer's accomplishments in other areas have been slighted because they once reported on sports.[36] Paul Gallico probably has become bet-ter known for writing *The Poseidon Adventure* than for anything he wrote on sports in the 1920s. The sportswriters who did not follow other pursuits are largely forgotten, confined to antholo-gies and a few dusty autobiographies.

Of this latter group, Grantland Rice may be the only Golden Age sportswriter remembered today by anyone outside the newspaper fraternity. Before the 1920s ended, Rice had become the first na-tionally famous sportswriter in the United States. He contributed regularly to national magazines such as *Collier's*, *Vanity Fair* and

Liberty. When he died in 1954, Rice remained the nation's most widely syndicated sports columnist.[37] For a sportswriter to be a hero maker, he must first reach an audience with his images. Rice reached more readers than any other writer of the Golden Age. His views on sports and athletes undoubtedly shaped public perception.

Writing in the *Nation* in 1921, theologian Reinhold Niebuhr, in hindsight, put his foot in his learned mouth with his thoughts about heroes just as the Golden Age of Sports was dawning: "Heroes can thrive only where ignorance reduces history to mythology. They cannot survive the coldly critical temper of modern thought when it is functioning normally, nor can they be worshipped by a generation which has every facility for detecting their foibles and analyzing their limitations."[38]

Perhaps modern thought was not functioning normally during the 1920s. Certainly one could cite examples of behavior that would make it seem so. The decade had an abundance of heroes, including several athletic legends who retain even today the luster as perhaps the greatest champions of their sports.

CHAPTER 3

Jack Dempsey

Grantland Rice never forgot what Jack Dempsey did to Jess Willard. He never got over the ferocity and power of Dempsey in his first heavyweight-championship victory against a much bigger opponent. He never let his readers forget either.

Dempsey met Willard for the title on July 4, 1919, in Toledo, Ohio. Dempsey had not yet been tagged the Manassa Mauler, but Willard, who stood six feet, six inches tall and weighed 245 pounds, deserved his nickname—the Pattawatomie Giant. The champion dwarfed the six-feet, one-inch tall, 191-pound challenger. Dempsey, however, decked Willard five times in the first round. By the third round, when Willard's handlers threw in the towel, the champion's face was cut to the bone in thirteen places and had swollen to twice its normal size.[1]

Rice credited Dempsey with unparalleled punching power because he inflicted such punishment on the hulking Willard. In his report on the fight for the *New York Tribune*, Rice called Dempsey "the hardest hitter the fight game has ever known." The superlatives began with the story's lead: "Jack Dempsey proved to be the greatest fighting tornado, in a boxing way, the game has ever known, when in nine minutes of actual combat today, he crushed Jess Willard into a shapeless mass of gore and battered flesh. . . . Never in all the history of the ring, dating back to days beyond all memory, has any champion ever received the murderous punishment which 245-pound Jess Willard soaked up in that first round and the two rounds that followed." Rice's story hailed Dempsey as "the most spectacular champion of them all."[2] This praise came less than a year after Dempsey had lost to the unexceptional Willie Meehan. Rice's image of Dempsey rested on the impression made by the pummeling of Willard.[3]

Dempsey won the heavyweight championship just as boxing gained wide popular appeal in the United States. Before World War I, most of the country considered boxing a brutal pastime surrounded by hooligans and gamblers. Many states had outlawed prizefighting. During the war, thousands of servicemen received instruction in boxing, creating more interest in the sport. After the war, the American Legion led the movement to bring down legal barriers to boxing, and the sport acquired a new respectability.[4] By the time Dempsey met Gene Tunney for the heavyweight title in 1926, the *New York Herald-Tribune* ran a list of 244 names of notables attending the bout under the headline "Many in Society Seen at Ringside."

Dempsey became the first beneficiary of the change in boxing's status. He had been a poor boy who had spent much of his life bouncing around the mining camps and ranch towns of the western United States. Rice blended the appealing rags-to-riches aspect of Dempsey's story with his discovery of the superhuman savage. Reporting on Dempsey's victory over Willard, Rice wrote: "With the championship now in plain sight, with the goal of his dreams just at the end of another hook, with all the world before him at 24—lifted from a tramp two years ago to a millionaire's income just ahead—he hooked those salvos of rights and lefts."[5]

The reference to a millionaire's income might have been a product of Rice's standard hyperbole. Previous heavyweight champions had not earned such exorbitant amounts of money. But in this instance, Rice proved prophetic. Perhaps Rice realized the implications of the change in boxing's status or knew fans would be drawn to see for themselves the superman he reported. Although gate receipts for the Dempsey-Willard fight totaled $452,000,[6] after

Jack Dempsey

Dempsey scored knockouts in his first two title defenses, five of his next six fights grossed more than one million dollars—the first million-dollar gates in boxing history. The sixth million-dollar gate did not occur until 1935, eight years after Dempsey's final fight.[7] Fans paid only $691,014 in 1928 to see the first postwar heavyweight title fight without Dempsey.[8]

Fans went to Dempsey's fights expecting mayhem from the wild man. But Rice also portrayed the champion as a sportsman having a more civilized side when not plying his craft: "Those who had seen [Dempsey] only in the ring looked upon him as a cave man. But those who knew him outside of the ring knew in him a certain personal attractiveness of manner, a certain magnetism, which made him many friends. . . . No one has ever heard Dempsey boast about beating an opponent or predict any knockout. His usual reply to such a question has always been: 'I don't know how it will end. I'll do my stuff.'"[9]

Dempsey modestly said of himself: "I was just a big kid that God blessed with a good punch. Besides that I had no other talents."[10] After beating Willard, Dempsey won three of his next four fights by knockout, but without the savage dominance exhibited in winning the title. On September 6, 1920, he knocked out Billy Miske, who was dying of Bright's disease, in the third round.[11] On December 14, 1920, Dempsey avoided losing his title in a decision with a twelfth-round knockout of Bill Brennan, who split open Dempsey's left ear. Rice described it as looking "like a cross between a veal cutlet breaded and a sponge dipped in gore."[12]

For Dempsey's third defense, promoter Tex Rickard used the champion's reputation as a boxing brute to hype the title fight with Georges Carpentier. The French challenger, who was really only a light-heavyweight, was portrayed as a literate, civilized man. Carpentier also had been decorated twice and wounded twice in the First World War, whereas Dempsey had not served in the war at all. With the foreigner-versus-American element added, the contrasts sparked a publicity that flamed into hysteria.[13]

Rice thought that the Dempsey-Carpentier hoopla was "badly overplayed, but eaten to the last adjective by the public."[14] The prefight publicity resulted in boxing's first million-dollar gate as 80,183 spectators in Jersey City, New Jersey, paid $1,789,283 to see Dempsey knock out Carpentier in the fourth round. The report of the fight crowded all the news off the front page of the *New York Times*, except for a small story about President Harding signing the document that officially ended the war. A Swiss daily, *Neue Zurcher Zeitung*, wrote that Dempsey's defeat of Carpentier symbolized that "the young democratic giant—as dramatically incorporated in Dempsey's powerful, brutal, natural strength, born of the American West—has become the master of the world."[15]

When Dempsey met another ring giant, Argentina's Luis Angel Firpo, on September 16, 1923, in New York, in his fifth title defense, Rice wrote that the boxers possessed between them "a greater amount of raw mule power in their fists than any other contending heavyweights of the decade." In the first round, Dempsey knocked down Firpo seven times, and "the Wild Bull of the Pampas" sent the champion to the canvas once and knocked him through the ropes into a row of sportswriters. The *Chicago Tribune*'s James Crusinberry called the opening round "the greatest round of battling since the Silurian Age."[16] In describing Dempsey's victory by a second-round knockout, Rice was more restrained than Crusinberry, but only a little. He wrote in the lead of his report for the *New York Tribune:* "In four minutes of the most sensational fighting ever seen in any ring through all the ages of the ancient game, Jack Dempsey, the champion, knocked out Luis Angel Firpo, the challenger, just after the second round got under way last night at the Polo Grounds. Dempsey slashed his way to victory with a right and a left to the jaw that lifted the Argentine giant from his feet and hurled him headlong to the floor with the crash of a mighty oak falling from great heights."[17]

Four years earlier, Rice had written that Willard "crashed to the sun-baked canvas with a thud that rolled forth the echo of his doom."[18] The reports of these two fights established Dempsey as a Jazz Age David, a real-life giant killer, even as a symbol of the spirit and strength of the United States in world affairs. After Dempsey defeated Firpo, the *Brooklyn Eagle* said in an editorial, "One shudders to think what might have happened to the Monroe Doctrine if Firpo had won. Today it is safe to say that South America has more respect for us than ever before. If Europe would only send over a first-class challenger, Mr. Dempsey might do something to restore American prestige abroad."[19]

More than three years passed after the Firpo bout before Dempsey fought again. In the interim, Rice wrote often of Dempsey, usually with the battered images of the giants Willard and Firpo in mind. Rice thought Dempsey's prowess rested on three factors: "speed of foot, terrific hitting with both hands, and unusual ring spirit. Practically discarding the use of any defense, he put the entire burden on attack."[20]

Like a carnivorous animal, Rice's Dempsey never ceased to attack his prey. In 1925, Rice asked: "Why is Jack Dempsey such an annihilating offensive machine? Partly because he is fast and because he can hit with either hand. But also because he has gone into action with a decisive line of thought, with his complete concentration upon a killing punch that may bring down his opponent to the floor. They have all hit him because he never thinks along defensive lines. He is willing to trade punches with anyone he meets, to take in order that he may give."[21] This strategy made Dempsey, in Rice's judgment in 1925, "the most annihilating champion in all of ring history. No one else has ever approached the deadliness and the ferocity of his attack."[22]

This image of Dempsey came into conflict with Rice's knowledge of boxing when the champion returned to the ring following a three-year layoff. Rice thought Dempsey's skills had rusted and wrote that "the odds will be against his beating any good man."[23] In an article for *Collier's*, Rice noted that periods of inactivity had preceded the title losses of all the previous heavy-

weight champions. "No athlete can make up for three years of retirement between the ages of 28 and 31. [Dempsey] may come back
to win, but there will be something missing," Rice reasoned.[24]

Yet less than a month before Dempsey fought again, Rice
wrote of him, "No one can take away from him the plain fact that
he is the fastest and the hardest two-handed hitter the heavyweight
division ever has known."[25] Rice conceded that after the long layoff, Dempsey would never be as he was against Willard, "hard
as a hydrant and as quick as a leopard." But Rice could not forget that Dempsey had "fists of iron."[26]

In his column for September 23, 1926, the day of Dempsey's return to the ring in a bout with Gene Tunney, Rice wrote, "Tunney
has never fought a ring battle yet that would whip Dempsey if he
happened to be within seventy percent of his best."[27] Dempsey lost
a ten-round decision to Tunney; but, even then, Rice could not
forget the fallen figures of the giants, Willard and Firpo. As the
rematch approached a year later, Rice argued with himself daily
in "The Sportlight" about the projected outcome: "All logic and reason whispers the name of Tunney. He made a crossword puzzle of
Dempsey's frontispiece just a year ago. . . . In spite of this I believe Dempsey has an even chance to win. I expect to see him
rush Tunney from the jump and I am not sure Tunney's jabs and
skill can keep him away."[28]

Rice thought Dempsey's spirit was willing: "More than anything else it is this flaming ring spirit that makes me figure him with
an even chance to win against all the laws and all the logic of the
ring."[29] And he did not think his flesh was weak either, how ever
skilled, cool, well-conditioned, and courageous Tunney might be:

> The memory of what Dempsey was may color one's judgment,
> but the fact remains that he looks about as formidable a fighting
> machine as any one would care to see.
>   If there is a surplus ounce on one of the most remarkable bod-
> ies in sport it doesn't show. He is sun-tanned and wind-tanned to

the color of copper, a fast, lean-looking fighter with his full share
of speed and stamina who is apparently possessed with the desire
to win and regain the old height he lost a year ago.

No fighter in ring history has worked harder over a two-year
stretch and at the end of his last training siege he is as ready for a
championship test as the human system can possibly be.[30]

Dempsey lost another ten-round decision to Tunney in perhaps
the most famous fight in boxing history. With a crowd of 105,000
spectators, who had paid a record gate of $2,658,660, looking on
in Chicago and 50 million fans listening on NBC radio, Dempsey
floored Tunney in the seventh round. Dempsey stepped away
from the fallen Tunney, but failed to go to a neutral corner as the
rules for the fight demanded. By the time referee Dave Barry directed Dempsey to the proper position, Tunney had spent an estimated five uncounted seconds on the canvas. Tunney rose at
the count of nine, but not before five radio listeners had died of
heart failure.[31]

Rice's fight story said nothing about the long count, only,
"Tunney got up at the count of nine, groggy. He was badly hurt."[32]
Rice's follow-up story did address the long count, but remember-
ing how Dempsey stood over Firpo and hammered him down
as he attempted to rise, he wrote, "Once in a while chickens come
home to roost." He thought that Dempsey had become "a victim
of old ring habits." Rice did not speculate on what would have
happened had Dempsey gone immediately to a neutral corner,
simply that he would have had a much better chance because
when he had thrown the big punch, "Tunney's mouth popped
open and his eyes had the look of a man badly hurt." Fittingly,
because this was Dempsey's last major fight, Rice ended the piece
as though writing Dempsey's obituary: "It will be a long, long time
before the ring gets another Manassa Mauler."[33]

Rather than decrease Dempsey's popularity, the loss of the
championship might have increased his appeal. Dempsey's reputa-

tion as a knockout artist and scowler contrasted with Tunney's fighting style and personality. Tunney nearly always had books with him at his training camps, and he projected an image of intellectual aloofness, quite unlike the stereotypical pug. Dempsey's one-punch solutions to his ring problems were more satisfying to fight fans than Tunney's style of defensive finesse. Rice reported on the crowd's reaction when Dempsey and Tunney were introduced while attending a fight between their two meetings: "Tunney was badly jolted to step into the ring at Madison Square Garden with Dempsey and find the ex-champ was on the popular end of the vocal reception. There were only cheers for Dempsey. There were about as many boos as cheers for Tunney."[34]

Although Rice helped build Dempsey's popularity and reputation through his stories, he also could write unflatteringly about Dempsey. Rice wrote more critically of Dempsey than of any other Golden Age hero. Unlike his contemporaries at the tops of the other popular sports, who seldom heard a discouraging word from the public, Dempsey went through periods of unpopularity.

A particular sore spot for Rice was Dempsey's failure to enlist during the war. Dempsey had received an exemption from the draft to support his wife, father, mother, and sister by working in a San Francisco shipyard, but he spent most of his time training and fighting. The first major sports event following the war's end was the Willard-Dempsey championship fight. Like Dempsey, Willard had remained a civilian during the war. Rice noted that four hundred reporters wrote more than six hundred thousand words on the fight, whereas twenty correspondents had sent back only fifty thousand words when the United States First Army had struck St. Mihiel less than a year earlier. He concluded that the thirty thousand ghosts in the Argonne Woods must be wondering what they had died for.[35] Rice expressed his feelings in the final paragraphs of his report on the fight for the *New York Tribune:*

For it would be an insult to every doughboy that took his heavy
pack through the mules' train to front line trenches to go over the
top at dawn to refer to Dempsey as a fighting man. If he had been
a fighting man he would have been in khaki when at twenty-two
he had no other responsibilities in the world except to protect his
own hide.

So let us have no illusions about our new heavyweight champion. He is a marvel in the ring, the greatest boxing or the greatest
hitting machine even the old-timers here have ever seen.

But he isn't the world's champion fighter. Not by a margin of
50,000,000 men who either stood, or were ready to stand the test
of cold steel and exploding shell for anything from six cents to a
dollar a day.

It would be an insult to every young American who sleeps
today from Flanders to Lorraine, from the Somme to the Argonne,
to crown Dempsey with any laurels of fighting courage.

He missed the big chance of his life to prove his own man-
hood before his own soul—but beyond that he stands today as the
ring marvel of the century, a puncher who will be unbeatable as
long as he desires to stay off the primrose way and maintain the
wonderful vitality of a wonderful human system.[36]

This first criticism of Dempsey set the pattern for the critical remarks
that followed. Even Rice's criticism often reinforced his image of
Dempsey. No matter how vexed Rice might get at Dempsey, the
criticism almost always carried a qualifier: this ring savage was
the puncher for the ages.

In preparation for his rematch with Tunney, Dempsey fought
Jack Sharkey on July 21, 1927. Dempsey won with a seventh-
round knockout. But Rice was among those who claimed Dempsey
set up his KO with a pair of low blows, then slugged Sharkey
senseless when his opponent doubled over in pain. In his report,
Rice wrote the two blows were "delivered a good eight inches
below the belt," Dempsey "fouled him twice plainly and openly
without any call from the referee," and "it was one of the most pal-

pable fouls any crowd ever looked upon." But the fair play–minded Rice really wasn't hard on Dempsey in his report. The story ended: "There have been few more savage fights up to the final punch. The supposedly war worn and rusty Dempsey was as full of battle as he ever was before. . . . He proved again his remarkable ability to take crushing punishment without going down, without giving up his endless pursuit of the younger and faster man. . . . It was regrettable, to put it mildly and to break it gently, that the fight ended under such a heavy and peculiar shadow."[37]

In his follow-up story, though, Rice began, "It evidently pays to be a drawing card." Rice had decided Dempsey could not be disqualified because that would ruin the financially lucrative rematch planned against Tunney later in the year.[38] Rice's strong contempt for the influence of money on sports guided his reporting. A week after the fight, Rice was still at it in his column:

[Dempsey] fouled Firpo all over the ring and he hit Sharkey low more than half a dozen times. He nailed Tom Gibbons low when Gibbons was halfway through the ropes at Shelby, and he also hit Gibbons more than once in that fight on the break.

This may be due to an overeager desire to belt your opponent, or it may be due to the knowledge that no one is around disqualifying a big gate attraction.

This is the golden age of sport, with the accent on the gold. It isn't so much the sporting age.[39]

Yet even amid such criticism, Rice realized that a savage did whatever it took to survive and inserted his qualifier: "There is no questioning Dempsey's ring spirit or his ring courage. There is no questioning his flame of battle with the leather hooked to his fins. He will stand as one of the durable sons of slug through all the records. He can take it and give it back."[40]

Of the athletic developments during the Golden Age, Rice least liked the growing commercialization of sports, as illustrated by his insinuations following the Dempsey-Sharkey fight. It conflicted with his view of athletics as fun and games and as a testing ground for spirit and courage.

When Dempsey's eight-year reign as heavyweight champion ended, Rice reflected on Dempsey's place in history, tackling the fans' favorite question, "Was he the greatest?" A week after Dempsey's second loss to Tunney, Rice assessed the former champion: "Dempsey, loaded up with ring courage and ring spirit, a slugging two-fisted walloper, backed up with remarkable durability and stamina, was his best against slow-moving targets only. . . . The good boxers gave him all his trouble."[41] An honest appraisal from a knowledgeable boxing observer, but not Rice's definitive word on Dempsey.

In a 1927 article for *Collier's* titled "Was Jack the Giant Killer?" Rice reported on his "long argument" with former heavyweight champion Jim Corbett on Dempsey's historical status. He reported that Corbett thought Dempsey did not rate high among the past champions except in the area of fighting spirit. Rice strongly disagreed: "It is my opinion that Jack Dempsey at his best was a great heavyweight, the most spectacular of them all if not actually the greatest. . . . Dempsey on that Toledo day was the greatest athlete that ever walked into any ring."[42] In the end Rice never left the beginning. In 1928, he wrote, "The Dempsey of Toledo was the most spectacular figure anyone ever saw in any ring. He was the most devastating annihilator of the entire lot. He had speed, terrific punching power and above all, the spirit of human destruction."[43]

The savage remained unbeatable. In the chapter devoted to Dempsey in Rice's 1954 autobiography, Rice put it this way: "In the ring he was a killer—a superhuman wild man. His teeth were frequently bared and his complete intent was an opponent's destruction."[44]

CHAPTER 4

Babe Ruth

Grantland Rice cried the first time he saw Babe Ruth. The tears didn't flow from oversentimentality, as some might suppose. Rice, suffering with a bad cold, met Ruth during spring training in 1919. Ruth pulled a raw onion from his pocket and offered it to Rice, his sure cure for the sportswriter's ailment. While Rice gnawed the onion with tears rolling down his face, he and Ruth struck up a friendship that would endure for the rest of their lives.[1]

Ruth needed friends in the press both less and more than any other of the sports heroes of the Golden Age. Ruth's baseball exploits were usually simple and Herculean enough to need no aggrandizement, although they received it in abundance. Soon after his playing ability grabbed the attention of the public, Ruth's often hedonistic life-style and unrefined personality became as much a part of the story as his home runs. Sportswriters chronicled both aspects of the Ruth legend.

Even in this period before electronic media, no one needed to unravel the secret to Ruth's success. He hit home runs like no one had hit them before. He hit them farther and more often, and even when others began to hit home runs, too, he remained the standard against which all others were measured.

When Rice met Ruth, the former star pitcher of the Boston Red Sox was preparing for his first season as an outfielder. Ruth held such hitting promise that the Red Sox decided to turn him into an everyday player after four seasons as a pitcher and part-time outfielder. Rice did not need much time to evaluate Ruth.

Even though Ruth had hit only twenty home runs in his major-league career, one week after the beginning of the 1919 baseball season, Rice presented his readers with the poem "Son of Swat—Babe Ruth":

When you can lean upon the ball
    And lay the seasoned ash against it,
The ball park is a trifle small,
    No matter how far out they've fenced it.
Past master of the four-base clout,
    You stand and take your wallop proudly —
A pretty handy bloke about,
    I'll say you are . . . and say it loudly.

I've seen a few I thought could hit,
    Who fed the crowd on four-base rations;
But you, Babe, are the only it—
    The rest are merely imitations.
I've seen them swing with all they've got
    And tear into it for a mop-up;
But what they deem a lusty swat
    To you is but a futile pop-up.

Somewhere amid another throng,
    Where Fate at times became unruly,
I've heard Big Bertha sing her song
    Without an encore for yours truly.
Yes, she had something—so to speak—
    A range you couldn't get away with,
But when you nail one on the beak
    They need another ball to play with.[2]

Ruth more than fulfilled Rice's expectations. He hit twenty-nine home runs, breaking the American League single-season record

Babe Ruth

of sixteen set by Socks Seybold in 1902. His total also passed the modern (post-1901) major-league record of twenty-four set by Gavvy Cravath in 1915 and the all-time major-league record of twenty-seven set by Edward Nagle Williamson in 1884.[3] But the twenty-nine home runs seemed more staggering than merely a new notation in the record book. Ruth hit more home runs than nine of the other fifteen big-league teams. The rest of his Red Sox teammates combined hit just four home runs.[4] He had reinvented baseball, or at least given an idea to those in position to do that.

Before Ruth began banging the ball into the bleachers, most batters choked up on their bats to punch hits, in the parlance of dead-ball giant Wee Willie Keeler, "where they ain't." Singles and stolen bases, not power hitting, ruled the offensive strategy in a low-scoring era. Attendance rose for all sixteen major-league teams in 1919. Some teams doubled or tripled their attendance figures of the war-shortened 1918 season. Some of the new fans may have had trouble appreciating the ascetic elegance of the strategic intricacies that governed the game, but all fans thrilled to the power of Ruth's home runs.

Excited by the windfall, the owners of baseball's teams were eager to give the fans what they wanted. Before the 1920 season, trick pitches such as the spitball were banned and umpires were directed to put new balls in play more often.[5] The resilience of the ball increased about this time because of a finer grade of wool wound tighter around its cork center.[6] Home-run production increased, but Ruth had not set off a complete chain reaction. He hit fifty-four home runs in 1920, a feat sportswriter Paul Gallico called "as incredible as the first heavier-than-air flying machine or the radio."[7] No team hit as many home runs as Ruth hit on his own that season.[8] All the teams except Detroit and Boston increased their attendance again, and Ruth's new club, the Yankees, drew nearly four hundred thousand more fans than any team had previously in a season.[9]

Following the 1919 season, Harry Frazee, the Red Sox owner who had a penchant for investing in Broadway flops, had sold

Ruth to the Yankees for $125,000 (more than twice the amount ever paid for a player previously) and a loan of $300,000. The announcement of the sale caused considerable consternation in Boston, which prompted Frazee to defend the deal. The Boston owner blamed Ruth for the Red Sox's sixth-place finish and said Ruth, who had held out for a higher-paying contract before the 1919 season started, had become impossible to manage and was one of the most selfish and inconsiderate men ever to play the game.[10] Rice thought this to be nonsense. He predicted Ruth would hit the unprecedented total of thirty-five or more home runs for the Yankees in 1920.[11]

Ruth set the standard in baseball for salary and public adulation, and other players began to emulate him and swing for the fences. In 1917, the major-league teams hits a total of 339 home runs; by 1922, that figure had increased to 1,055.[12] From 1910 to 1919, players reached 100 runs batted in during a season 27 times; from 1920 through 1929, that feat was accomplished 142 times. The number of no-hit games decreased from 32 to 9 during those same time periods.[13]

Ruth's home runs needed no interpretation for the fans, but the sportswriters gave them plenty of description. Ruth hit 714 regular-season home runs, a record Rice considered "beyond anybody's reach unless they use rubber balls and crowd the fences towards the infield."[14] Ruth hit fifteen more home runs in World Series play. In the newspapers, hardly any of these 729 home runs seemed merely to land politely beyond the outfield fence. Those hit during the World Series garnered the most attention, and Ruth had plenty of opportunities in the spotlight: the Yankees won the American League pennant six times between 1921 and 1929 and again in 1932. Because Rice did not cover the Yankees on a daily basis, he saw more of Ruth while covering the World Series.

Against St. Louis in 1926, Ruth became the first player to hit three home runs in a World Series game. The feat sent Rice reaching for larger-than-life imagery and mythological allusions. His report on the game began:

After the manner of a human avalanche hurtling on its downward way from the blue Missouri heavens the giant form of Babe Ruth fell upon the beleaguered city of St. Louis to-day and flattened it into a pulp of anguish.

If another mighty planet had slipped its ancient moorings to come crashing through unlimited space against the rim of the earth it could not have left one sector in its path more dismantled or forlorn . . .

An enraged bull in a china shop of fragile bric-a-brac would be a mere kitten playing with yarn compared to the astonishing infant who lashed the ball over the stands into Grand Avenue twice and then hammered another home run into the center field seats 430 feet away, for the first time in Missouri history . . .

It is just a picture of a large portly form taking a wild cut at the ball and then loafing along the open highway with a stunned and startled crowd wondering who let old Doc Thor or the bolt-heaving Jupiter into the show. It was smash-smash-smash and then a steady, even unhurried trot from the plate back to the plate with the ball bounding on its way down St. Louis thoroughfares through brokenhearted crowds.[15]

A batter swinging the hammer of Thor could not be expected to hit ordinary home runs. Ruth did not, at least according to the descriptions of Rice: "His third St. Louis home run was practically a line drive, yet it was still moving at hurricane speed when it crashed into the crowd on the seats 450 feet from the plate. It certainly would have traveled more than 500 feet before hitting the ground if there had been no stand."[16] Later in that series, Ruth showed his long-ball versatility by belting a different kind of four-bagger: "It was a home run that cracked all altitude records for a batted ball for at the crest of its flight the ball resembled a buckshot hung from the sky."[17]

In the next year's World Series, Ruth returned to impressive line-drive home runs. Rice described Ruth's home run in the third game against the Pirates in the 1927 World Series this way: "There was no fuzz of any sort to this hit. It left a trail of smoke in its wake as it spun about 15 feet above the ground into the massed humanity of the right field section. The racket that greeted Mr. Ruth's smooth and mighty swing, which scored three runs in a lump, is still said to be echoing on its way across the New England hills."[18]

So much was expected of Ruth that even his off days became news. In his story on the Yankees' second victory in the four-game sweep of Pittsburgh in 1927, Rice used three of the first six paragraphs detailing the fact that Ruth had been held hitless. Ruth seemed more the story than the outcome of the game as Rice summarized the Yankee outfielder's day: "With the Pirates licked to a faint whisper the big crowd began to pin its hope for excitement on Babe Ruth. There was a flood of excitement every time he came to bat, a wild flutter of renewed interest in another dull ball game, but the Babe was as helpless as the submerged Pirates. He couldn't hit the size of his hat."[19]

Reaching batting marks previously unattainable became so commonplace for Ruth that sometimes the same group that went wild over his home runs took his other feats in stride. His mark of 60 home runs hit during the 1927 season became a hallowed record, so much so that when Roger Maris broke the single-season home-run mark with 61 homers in 1961, baseball commissioner Ford Frick decreed that Maris's mark would carry an asterisk to indicate that he had accomplished the feat in a 162-game season, compared to the 154-game slate of Ruth's time. But in 1927, Ruth's sixtieth home run did not cause the commotion that one might associate with the event, even though it broke his 1921 record of 59 homers. Expectations were that Ruth would hit even more the following year.[20]

Any superlatives one might want to use about Ruth's ability seemed appropriate. After all, how many players had a ball park built for them? In 1923, the Yankees opened Yankee Stadium, built with the money Ruth had brought their way by attracting record-breaking attendance and to hold the crowds Ruth would draw in the future as he hit home runs out of a field designed to favor a left-handed pull hitter (i.e., Ruth). Aptly, Yankee Stadium was known as the House that Ruth Built. The first game there drew 74,217 spectators, to that time the largest crowd to see a baseball game.[21]

Not all the Yankees' money went into building the ball park—Ruth earned the unheard-of salary of fifty-two thousand dollars in 1922, a time when a family man could live comfortably on eighty dollars a month. As a well-paid, veteran star, third baseman Frank Baker, whose nickname Home Run now seemed misplaced, had the second-highest Yankee salary at sixteen thousand dollars.[22]

Rice often pointed out, though, that the Yankees got more for their money than the power hitter who set single-season records that still stand for highest slugging percentage, most total bases, most extrabase hits, most runs, and most walks.[23] Ruth was an all-around star, not just a home-run hitter, according to a 1926 column by Rice: "If Ruth had been a light hitter he would have been ranked as a remarkable defensive star. From the combination of outfield range, handling ground balls and pegging to the plate there have been few better in baseball history. But the big blow is more impressive, and so overshadows technique along other lines not quite so showy."[24]

Sometimes, though, the Yankees got even more than a complete ballplayer for their money. They also got trouble. At times, Ruth seemed to live up to the earlier assessment of Red Sox owner Frazee that he was impossible to manage. Following the 1921 World Series, Ruth and Yankee teammate Bob Meusel participated in a barnstorming tour without the permission of the baseball commissioner. Kenesaw Landis fined both players about the amount of their World Series shares and suspended them until May 20 of the 1922 season. Later that season, Ruth was fined and stripped of his duties as the Yankees' captain for throwing dirt into an umpire's face and climbing into the stands to fight a heckler. He followed that with two three-game suspensions for run-ins with umpires. After the season ended, Ruth promised to reform and came back to win the American League Most Valuable Player Award in 1923.[25]

Ruth's popular image rested on not only his excesses with the bat but also his excessive appetites off the field for everything from soda pop, hot dogs, and steak to alcohol, women, and night life. In 1925, Ruth's life-style, always a topic of interest for the newspapers, collided in the press with his baseball career when he went down with "the bellyache heard 'round the world." Ruth collapsed April 8 in spring training, spent the next few weeks in hospitals in North Carolina and New York, and underwent surgery for the removal of an intestinal abscess. He did not return to the field until June. The season marked the only time during Ruth's career with New York that the Yankees finished worse than third place, coming in twenty-eight and a half games behind the pennant-winning Washington Senators. Ruth played in ninety-eight games and managed twenty-five home runs.[26]

Rice was not among those who thought Ruth had burned out for good. In August he wrote, "There are many who believe the Babe is about through, but there is not reason for any such belief, if he has learned his lesson . . . he may still return to the throne which he had to surrender this spring and summer."[27] Two weeks after writing those words, Rice's confidence seemed ill placed. Miller Huggins, the Yankees manager, fined Ruth five thousand dollars and suspended him indefinitely for misconduct on and off the field. Ruth's suspension lasted from August 30 to September 8.[28] Later, Rice wrote of Huggins's problems handling his star player: "In Ruth, Miller had two tigers by their tails, for Babe would accept a five thousand-dollar fine and a long suspension with a grin."[29] Ruth did nothing of the sort in this instance. When his bluster ran out, he came back to the Yankees, and Rice spent many column inches in the off-season telling of

Ruth's contrite rededication to the game. In December, Rice reported to readers that Ruth was training already to return to the top of the big leagues in home runs. Rice joked about Ruth's past troubles, "The Babe suddenly discovered he couldn't eat his cake and have his home runs, too."[30]

Ruth's appetite for things of the flesh became well known, but the stories of Ruth's off-the-field exploits during his career often were vague and short on specific circumstances, except for anecdotes about prodigious eating feats, especially when they were followed shortly by baseball heroics. Rice pioneered the general picture of Ruth as a happy-go-lucky, uncultured man-child. In a 1925 *Collier's* piece, Rice compared Ruth to former heavyweight boxing champion John L. Sullivan, writing that both men were profane, blunt, and raw; made no attempt to conceal their rough edges; and disliked training and discipline.[31]

As a good friend, Rice knew plenty about Ruth's less-exemplary off-the-field activities, but he wrote little of them during Ruth's lifetime. When Ruth died in 1948, Rice wrote:

> The true story of Babe's life will never be written—the story of wrecked cars he left along the highway—the story of the night he came near dropping Miller Huggins off a train—the story of the $100,000 or more he lost in Cuba one racing winter.
>
> The story of the ribald, carefree Babe who ignored all traffic signals . . .
>
> He was a rough, rowdy swaggering figure, more profane than anyone I ever hope to meet again, with a strong sense of decency and justice and fair play.

In the main, Rice concentrated his off-the-field stories about Ruth on these last facets of Ruth's character, the friendly man who called every older man "Pop," every older woman "Mom," and everybody else "Kid." This was the beloved Babe who supposedly said, "Hi, Prez! Hot as hell, ain't it?" upon being introduced to President Coolidge. Stories describing Ruth and a friend shooting at a door knob with a .22-caliber rifle in a golf club at a wager of one dollar per shot and Ruth nearly shooting an unsuspecting man who opened the door ("He should have knocked," Ruth said) were not as frequent in Rice's work as those of Ruth putting his time to more constructive use. If Rice's stories are an accurate guide, whatever feelings Ruth might have had for hot dogs, beer, and women, he loved two things more—baseball and children. In Ruth's obituary, Rice wrote of accompanying Ruth on a sixty-mile drive to visit a sick boy on the eve of a World Series game in Chicago. Ruth warned Rice, "And if you write anything about it, I'll knock your brains out."[32]

Rice followed Ruth's wishes, but he wrote of many other instances in which Ruth helped children, either with visits, gifts, or financial assistance. Third baseman Joe Dugan has said that on his first day as a Yankee, Ruth walked into the clubhouse and gave a huge stack of mail to Dugan with instructions to "put the letters from the broads in one pile and the ones with the checks in the other. Throw the other junk away, especially the sappy stuff from fans."[33] That contrasts with Rice's description of Ruth in 1925, the time when his character was most in question, as someone who had "spent innumerable hours going out of his way to help youngsters singly and in groups, to take them autographed baseballs, to help pay their doctors' bills."[34]

The front page of the *New York Herald-Tribune* that proclaimed Ruth's feat of three home runs in one World Series game in 1926 also carried the headline "Ruth Keeps Air Mail Promise of Homer for Boy Near Death." Ruth had sent the message, "I'll knock a homer for you in Wednesday's game," along with baseballs autographed by the Cardinals and Yankees, to critically ill Johnny Sylvester, an eleven-year-old in Essex Falls, New Jersey.[35] Rice later wrote, "Babe's love of kids was sincere. In many ways he was a big kid himself."[36] A big kid playing a kid's game and making a lot of money at it. "He has made a fortune at baseball, but the crowd could see that he was playing the game for fun above all else," Rice wrote in 1925.

Fans might have wondered, however, how much fun Ruth could have on the field, because he sometimes had to perform with nearly crippling injuries, according to Rice's reports. In the 1922 World Series against the Giants, Ruth played "with an infected arm swollen to twice its normal size and one leg just about hanging on. He was a double cripple in leg and arm, risking the loss of both by further injury, yet nothing could keep him off the field."[37] In a big series against Detroit in 1924, Ruth again had a double injury: "Either wound would have been enough to stop the ordinary mortal and send him to the hospital for repairs. But neither the pain nor the handicap diverted Ruth's attention from the main business at hand nor broke down his determination to fight it out."[38] In 1926, "Ruth had the greatest all-around season of his career, a slam bang hitting campaign that carried the Yankees through and a big defensive march in spite of injuries that would have driven the ordinary mortal to the hospital."[39]

Rice had a ready explanation for how Ruth, apparently no ordinary mortal, was able to play through these injuries—a heroic love for baseball. Near the end of Ruth's record-breaking 1927 season, Rice wrote: "About the only way one can account for his latest showing after 14 years of service is his love for the game. The Babe could never buy as much fun with a million dollars as he gets out of baseball. He will be a lost soul when his career is over, for nothing else will ever take baseball's place in his walloping existence."[40] As happened so often, history proved Rice correct. Nothing ever did take baseball's place in Ruth's life. Between his retirement in 1935 and his death from cancer in 1948, Ruth seemed more a national monument than a person.

When Ruth died, Rice neatly summarized the enormous twin appeal of the Babe—his baseball ability and his unaffected personality. "The greatest figure the world of sport has ever known has passed from the field. Game called on account of darkness. Babe Ruth is dead," Rice's column began. He went on to write, "Ruth was the greatest all-around ballplayer in the history of the game. . . . No other athlete ever approached his color, not even the colorful Jack Dempsey, who had more than his share. . . . No game will ever see his like, his equal again. He was one in many, many lifetimes. One all alone."[41]

CHAPTER 5

Bobby Jones

Television viewers can occasionally see Bobby Jones's fluid golf swing and hear his equally rhythmic Georgia drawl even though more than sixty years have passed since he capped his competitive career by becoming the only golfer to win four major championships in one season. A series of eighteen films made by Jones in 1931 and 1932 has been converted to videocassettes and is being hawked to compete with tapes divulging the scoring secrets of modern players in the instructional golf market. In a series of vignettes, Jones demonstrates for entertainers such as W. C. Fields, James Cagney, Edward G. Robinson, and Douglas Fairbanks, Jr., how best to handle the hickory-shafted clubs of his time.

The promotional advertisements for the tapes advise buyers to learn from "the greatest golfer of all-time." The tag line smacks of salesmanship, yet it holds a certain credibility, in spite of the exploits of Byron Nelson, Ben Hogan, Arnold Palmer, and Jack Nicklaus since Jones roared through the 1920s and won the grand slam in 1930. Grantland Rice, undoubtedly, would agree wholeheartedly with the sales pitch. In fact, he may have been the first to make the claim. Rice spent nearly thirty years proclaiming Jones not only the greatest golfer the game had ever had but also the greatest it could ever have.

Jones won his first major golf championship in 1923 by beating Bobby Cruickshank on the eighteenth hole of their playoff in the U.S. Open. Although Jones had made his debut in the top echelon of golf seven years earlier in the U.S. Amateur and had played in three previous U.S. Open tournaments without winning, Rice took Jones down the first step to immortality. After Jones's playoff victory, Rice wrote for the *New York Tribune*, "Beyond any question he deserves the title as the greatest golfer of his day." Rice used statistics to justify the claim, a rarity for him. Rice noted that over the last four U.S. Open tournaments, Jones had finished with a cumulative score fourteen strokes better than Walter Hagen, the leading professional player of the time.[1]

The next year, Jones won the U.S. Amateur championship for the first time. The victory came much easier than Jones's first major championship. In the match-play final, Jones recorded the tournament's widest victory margin since 1895 as he led George Von Elm by ten holes with eight to play when the match ended. After Jones's second victory in a national-championship tournament, Rice added to his praise from the previous year: "The most brilliant golfer in the world, the essence of rhythm, style, and form, is on top at last in a game where the odds are always overpowering."[2]

Rice's praise of Jones as the best golfer of his time might seem premature. But so might Rice's early pronouncements on Babe Ruth and others. Many top players and observers of golf at the time thought Jones had the skill to win at the national-championship level before he finally broke through at Inwood in 1923. He had shown improvement in each of his outings in the U.S. Open, finishing eighth in 1920, fifth in 1921, and second in 1922. Yet he also had played in ten national championships before winning the 1923 U.S. Open and required a playoff to secure that title after stumbling through the final three holes of the fourth round in sixteen strokes.[3]

After winning the 1924 U.S. Amateur championship to go with a second-place finish in the U.S. Open that year, Jones had established himself as one of the top golfers in the country. His seemingly flawless swings might have been worthy of Rice's super-

Bobby Jones

latives, but his credentials did not appear to set him apart as "the greatest golfer of his day" and "the most brilliant golfer in the world."

By the time Jones earned his second national title with the 1924 U.S. Amateur victory, Hagen had won the U.S. Open, the British Open, and the U.S. Professional Golfers' Association Championship twice each. (Considered a major championship tournament today, the PGA started in 1916 and was played for only the third time in 1920.) In 1922, Hagen became the first United States native to win the British Open, the foremost tournament of the time. Hagen also was a favorite of Rice's. Hagen was glib, outgoing, a free spender with a love for night life—the kind of athlete about whom Rice liked relating anecdotes. British Open officials went so far as to ask Hagen to change clothes in the caddy shack; as a professional he wasn't welcome in the clubhouse. Hagen directed his chauffeur to drive to the clubhouse door, where he changed clothes in the back seat of his limousine. He went on to win the British Open twice more and the PGA title three more times before the 1920s ended. Many experts still consider Hagen the finest match-play golfer in history.

Gene Sarazen stood as Hagen's stiffest professional competition. Sarazen had finished ahead of Bobby Jones at the top of the 1922 U.S. Open field. He also won the PGA championship that year and the next. Francis Ouimet, Jones's top competitor for honors as the country's leading amateur golfer, had won as many national championships as Jones. As a twenty-year-old, Ouimet defeated British stars Harry Vardon and Ted Ray to win the 1913 U.S. Open. Ouimet's victory sparked the greatest burst of enthusiasm for golf in the United States to that time. Ouimet also won the U.S. Amateur championship in 1914, a feat he repeated in 1931, the year after Jones's retirement.[4]

Even with these other luminaries in the golf world, Rice seemed to have no doubt that it was Jones who deserved the praise as the greatest golfer of the era. He was nearly ready to declare Jones the greatest golfer of all time when Jones repeated as U.S. Amateur champion in 1925 after consecutive second-place finishes in the previous two U.S. Open tournaments. Rice qualified his praise by calling Jones "the greatest amateur golfer at match and medal play combined the game has ever known."[5] Because most of the golfers who had preceded Jones had been amateurs, this came close to a declaration for Jones as the greatest golfer ever.

In the last half of the decade, Jones made Rice appear an astute judge of golfing ability to have promoted him into greatness with so little evidence. After Jones won the U.S. Amateur championship in 1927 for his fourth major title in two years, Rice, in a story for the *New York Herald-Tribune* that seems written with solemn glee, declared Jones as the greatest golfer since a Scot first struck a ball with a cudgel: "Bobby Jones through the course of this championship proved beyond all question that he is the greatest golfer that ever lived. You will hear about the wizardry of Vardon and Taylor, of Travers and Hagen, but in the span of time that dates back 500 years there has been only one Jones."[6]

Yet even the greatest can get better, it seems. As an amateur who played in only a few tournaments each season, Jones usually readied himself informally for championship play. In 1930, however, he entered two tournaments to tune up, finishing second in the Savannah Open and winning by thirteen strokes the Southeastern Open in Augusta, Georgia. Rice watched Jones's Southeastern victory. Afterward he said Jones was playing discernibly better than ever before.

Again, Rice had Jones handicapped much better than the daily-double horses on which he habitually lost money. By this time everyone else had come to agree with Rice that Jones was the greatest golfer of the era. Only diehards still held out for Vardon as the best in history. In 1930, Jones proved discernibly better than he had been before and certainly better than any of his competition. He won the four major championships—the amateur and open titles of the United States and Great Britain. No other golfer has ever accomplished golf's grand slam.

The grand slam ended a remarkable eight-year period of championship golf that started for Jones with his victory in the 1923 U.S. Open. He won that tournament three more times and finished second three times, twice losing in playoffs. He won the U.S. Amateur championship five times and finished second once. He won the British Open all three times he played in it. Jones played only twice during this period in the grueling British Amateur, a championship consisting of seven rounds of eighteen-hole matches followed by a thirty-six hole, match-play final. Jones had reached the fifth round in 1926 before his 1930 victory.

Jones's accomplishments make his own attitude about his skills seem modest compared to Rice's assessment. In his 1927 autobiography *Down the Fairway*, Jones called the chapter on 1926 "The Biggest Year" because he thought he would never have another chance to win both the British and U.S. Open championships in the same year.[7] Rice's superlatives began at such an exalted point that he had to stretch further and further for terms of admiration as the golfer's achievements mounted through the 1920s. In 1924, when Jones whipped Von Elm for his first U.S. Amateur championship, he "became a flaming meteor tearing across the heavens of golf. Whatever he struck became dust."[8]

After winning the Open championships of the United States and Great Britain in 1926, Jones attempted to become the first golfer to win three major titles in one year in the U.S. Amateur. When Jones defeated Chick Evans in the quarterfinal round, Rice began his *New York Herald-Tribune* story, "They have started calling him Emperor Jones, but he must be something more than a mere emperor. An emperor wears one crown. Jones is already wearing two and he is only two golf matches away from a third. This ought to make him something which the historical records have never thought about."[9] In his semifinal victory over Ouimet, "Jones was a package of dynamite, gun cotton and TNT combined. . . . He made golf look as simple as lifting a hat or waving to a friend."[10] In the championship match, though, Jones missed a seven-foot putt on the thirty-fifth hole to lose to Von Elm, whom he had routed in the tournament in the previous two years. Rather than concentrate on the sudden failure of Jones's putter, "Calamity Jane," Rice wrote of the fine pitch that preceded the missed putt: "Under all conditions it was a great shot that only a champion could play, for it still gave him another chance to defend his two-year crown." Jones didn't lose; Von Elm beat him in a once-in-a-career show of skill and spirit: "It was not that Jones failed. In this case one must give credit to the great skill of Von Elm's wood and iron and to the shining flame in his soul."[11]

Jones regained the U.S. Amateur championship the next year a few weeks after his worst performance ever in the U.S. Open— a tie for eleventh place. Jones's slip in one national championship did not deter Rice's admiration of his performance in the other. Rice's story on the U.S. Amateur began: "Once or twice within the course of a century a prodigy comes along to ride the crest of the world. He may be a Rembrandt or a Galileo or a Shakespeare. He may be a DaVinci or a Milton. But there is about him an indefinable touch of mastery that lifts him far above the puny achievements of even the near great. Golf has contributed its addition to the galaxy of masters in the person of Robert Tyre Jones Jr. of Atlanta."

Jones had shot a record score in the British Open earlier in the summer and set a course record in the morning round of the U.S. Amateur championship final. The way Rice describes Jones's play, one wonders how opponent Chick Evans managed to last twenty-nine holes, because he "never had a chance against the modern Merlin who waved a magic wand that drove par into the background and made perfect golf as the human knows it, look crude and listless. . . . (Jones) smothered Chick Evans with a barrage of wood and steel that no golfer in the history of the game could have faced." Perhaps Rice could think of no finer praise than to cite other Golden Age heroes, because he ended his story, "For here was a combination of Tilden, Hitchcock, Ruth, Nurmi and

Grange, all in one blend of power and skill, grace and rhythm, form and results."[12]

Jones's most famous single shot came in his first major victory, the 1923 U.S. Open. On the final hole of the final round, Jones took a double-bogey six and Bobby Cruickshank carded a birdie to force an eighteen-hole playoff for the championship. The next day, the two golfers came to the eighteenth tied at seventy-two and put their drives in the rough. Cruickshank cautiously played his second shot short of the water guarding the green. But Jones lashed a two-iron through the rough and knocked his ball 190 yards to within eight feet of the cup. Rice wrote of the gallery's roar: "It was tribute to a heart stout enough to trample psychology and imagination into the dust and come through at the big moment upon the same shot that had yielded bitterness and disaster only days before." Rice thought the shot a superb demonstration of skill and spirit. He began his *New York Tribune* account:

> The red badge of courage always belongs upon the breast of the fighter who can break and then come back with a stouter heart than he ever had before.
>
> This crimson decoration of valor came to Robert Tyre Jones, of Atlanta, 21-year-old amateur, when he rode at last yesterday to the crest of the open golf championship of the United States on one of the greatest iron shots ever played in the game that goes back through 500 years of competitive history.[13]

Jones was an outstanding golfer, possibly a superman on the links. Rice wrote at length on Jones's inherent powers and abilities, if not actually proclaiming the golfer as something more than a mortal man. In 1927, Rice wrote for *Collier's:* "He was born with the capacity for great concentration and determination and above all with a remarkable blend of mental and muscular rhythm which a thousand years of training might not have brought to another."[14] Sometimes Jones seemed more machine than man, as

Rice wrote later, "There is nothing to be done when you step out against a golfer who drives 280 to 300 yards down the middle, plants his next shot 4, 7 or 10 feet from the cup and holes most of the putts."[15]

This dehumanizing of the athletic stars of the 1920s by the sports press has become one of the criticisms of sports writing in the Golden Age, with Rice unfairly lumped with his imitators. Robert Lipsyte has written:

> Painting a lily is not only presumptuous, but ultimately destructive. The flower dies. By layering sports with pseudo-myth and fakelore, by assigning brutish or supernatural identities to athletes, the Rice-ites dehumanized the contests and made objects of the athletes.
>
> The writer who criticizes a ballplayer for muffing a grounder, no matter how nasty he gets about it, is still dealing with the ballplayer within his context. He is judging the athlete as a working professional. But the writer who likens a ballplayer to Hercules or Grendel's mother is displaying the ultimate contempt—the ballplayer no longer exists as a person or a performer, but as an object, a piece of matter to be used, in this case, for the furtherance of the sportswriter's career by pandering to the emotional titillation of the reader/fan. Rice populated the press boxes with lesser talents who insisted, like the old master, that they were just sunny fellows who loved kids' games and the jolly apes who played them.[16]

However much of a superman Rice portrayed Jones as being on the course, he often reminded readers that Jones had had to overcome a common human failing to become a champion. Although the picture of a southern gentleman in his dealings with opponents and fans, Jones directed a terrible temper against himself. Rice told his readers he had watched Jones battle against himself for seven years, from his national debut in the 1916 U.S. Amateur to his victory in the 1923 U.S. Open, trying to harness a temperament more suited for "some fast-moving game where aggressiveness is a factor," such as football or tennis. Jones always had the skill to win, Rice wrote, but he would tighten his grip and hurry his backswing after playing a bad stroke or when facing an important shot. By 1923, Jones had gained the self-control needed to allow his talent to triumph: "He had won his fight. From that point on, one might watch him after playing a bad hole or after a poor stroke and see a smooth, even, unhurried swing that carried no hint of the trouble that had gone before. . . . It was his persistent and finally successful battle for mastery of self that made the vast difference."[17]

Rice also let readers know that whatever natural gifts Jones possessed, he had honed those endowments with an early start and hard work. Rice liked to tell of the small boy with the oversized head who could imitate precisely the unhurried swing of Stewart Maiden, the Scottish pro at the Atlanta Athletic Club, where Jones's family lived just off the thirteenth fairway of the East Lake Course: "It was in the early stages of his career, back in the true imitative age, that he laid the foundation for a golf swing not only entirely correct, but almost entirely intuitive and subconscious."[18]

The combination of natural talent and determination allowed Jones to be something more than a good golfer in Rice's formula for greatness: "Genius combines gifts from the gods with an even rarer quality—the ability to develop and realize on natural endowment. . . . Robert Tyre Jones, Second, of Atlanta, Georgia, was the complete human pattern for supreme genius."[19]

Jones did not project any more color than these stories could impart to him. After taming his temperamental drive for perfection, he stood as a model of deportment and restraint on the course. He had none of the pizzazz of Hagen, but he was enormously popular anyway, leaving record-sized galleries trampling courses in his wake. Jones's popularity rubbed off on his sport. In 1920, the United States Golf Association had 477 mem-

ber clubs. By 1930, the USGA had 1,154 member clubs, and the
United States had more than 5,700 golf courses.[20]

Although Jones possessed a workmanlike demeanor that resulted in lyrical golf, Rice helped popularize the game with verses
of his own. An ardent golfer, Rice contributed "Tales of a Wayside Tee," a second column that dealt only with golf, to the *New
York Herald-Tribune*. He often ended his "Sportlight" with a few
paragraphs under the heading "To-day's Golf Lesson." Rice gave
the sense that golf is fun through his short poems about the game,
such as in "Any Golf Championship" and the first verse of "So It
Goes," both outcries against the mystery and misery of putting:

> I'm driving straight and my irons are good;
> I'm getting home as a winner should;
> I'm down the middle every sock,
> And I ought to win by a city block.
> I'm on the pin when I see the green,
> Moving on like a young machine;
> You orter see my half-iron pokes,
> I orter lead by a dozen strokes—
> ButthehellofitisIain'tputtin.
>
> A long straight drive with a forward spin—
> A long straight iron to the waiting pin—
> An iron that clears all traps and ruts—
> Then you take three putts.[21]

Jones's appeal might have resulted from the way he combined overpowering talent with a certain winning gallantry. Amateur golfers
had been considered affluent dandies in most of the United States
before Jones became the country's foremost sportsman, a well-man-
nered, fair play–minded, gracious winner who kept the three-inch
cup he won in a tournament for those ten and younger alongside
his trophies from the world's major golf championships.[22] Rice prob-

ably did not find these characteristics so remarkable. He had played collegiate baseball against Jones's father, Colonel Bob Jones, was a friend of the family, and had known Bobby since he was a baby. As a like-minded southerner of the era, Rice simply expected such behavior from someone with Jones's background.[23]

Others made more of a fuss over Jones's behavior. Paul Gallico, who thought the Golden Age would have been golden even had it produced only Jones, wrote, "Probably no celebrity in sport ever attracted quite so much attention and was so dominating a figure and yet remained completely unspoiled."[24] Even sportswriter John R. Tunis, who often wrote critically of Rice's heroes, wrote of Jones, "It is no accident that Mr. Robert T. Jones is almost the only champion in any branch of sport who is genuinely popular with those who play against him and, therefore, see him under the stress of modern competition. The strain at the top is too great for most men."[25]

The strain at the top ultimately proved too much for even Jones. But this did not cause him to throw his clubs, demean opponents, and abuse galleries. Instead, after winning the Grand Slam at the age of twenty-eight, he retired from championship competition. The calmness Jones possessed while addressing his ball sometimes were the only moments of serenity he experienced during tournaments, when he could lose as many as twelve pounds.[26]

Jones also had done all an amateur could do in golf, and his law career in Atlanta had begun to take up increasing amounts of his time. In 1926, Rice wrote that Jones had twenty to twenty-five years left in championship golf and speculated that he would win the U.S. Amateur more than the eight times John Ball had captured the British Amateur championship.[27] But Rice considered the grand slam "a record that will challenge time itself,"[28] so Jones withdrew from the game with his blessing, a king with no frontiers to subdue rather than a monarch weary of the weight of the crown: "He saw no more worlds to conquer. At best, there could be nothing but anticlimax left. . . . So Bobby Jones wisely retired."[29]

Rice continued to write about Jones after his retirement, once relating the events of a friendly round he and Jones had played at St. Andrews during a visit to Great Britain. He described how word of mouth spread the news that Jones was playing, and how by the end of the round, Rice and Jones had a gallery of six thousand spectators, including an old Scot with tears of joy streaming into his beard. Rice wrote of the experience: "Whatever any future giant of the links does to par, nobody will ever replace Robert Tyre Jones in the hearts of those to whom golf is something more than a game."[30]

Of course, future giants did arise, but golf was something more than a game to Rice, and nobody ever replaced Jones in his heart. Before Rice's death in 1954, he had the opportunity to marvel at the golfing skill of Ben Hogan, who had recovered from a near-fatal automobile accident in 1949 to become one of the best players in history. During Rice's lifetime, Hogan won the U.S. Open four times, the Masters and PGA twice each, and the British Open in his only appearance in that tournament. From 1940 to 1960, Hogan never finished out of the top ten in the U.S. Open, and from 1941 to 1956, he placed at least in the top seven at the Masters.[31]

Rice admired and liked Hogan. He wrote that Hogan had more dedication than any athlete he had seen.[32] Yet it always would be futile to compare any golfer to Jones, as Rice wrote for the *Saturday Evening Post:* "There is no more chance that golf will give the world another Jones than there is that literature will produce another Shakespeare, sculpture another Phidias, music another Chopin. There is no more probability that the next 500 years will produce another Bobby than there is that two human beings will be born with identical fingerprints."[33]

CHAPTER 6

Bill Tilden

Grantland Rice thought the sports fans of the Golden Age loved offense. A powerful attack, what he liked to call "wallop," lay at the base of the appeal of the athletic idols of the period, he thought. Boxing fans were cool to Gene Tunney because of his strategic, defensive style of fighting; they preferred his predecessor, Jack Dempsey, whom Rice portrayed as a single-minded destroyer in the ring. Red Grange's ability to jolt the opposition with a touchdown run from any spot on the field made him the football hero of the age. The tape-measure home runs of Babe Ruth and the screaming tee shots of Bobby Jones grabbed the attentions of the fans in baseball and golf.

Even tennis, which before the First World War had been an isolated and genteel pursuit, had an "Apostle of Punch" in the 1920s. "The most appealing factor in any sport is the roar of the heavy artillery," Rice wrote, and he counted the searing serves of Bill Tilden among the heaviest field pieces in sports.[1] Tilden could boom serves at 151 miles per hour even at the age of forty.[2]

In a scene Rice re-created several times for his readers, Tilden needed one game to win his fifth consecutive U.S. singles championship. But a rumble of thunder threatened a storm that would interrupt the match with Little Bill Johnston, the perennial tennis bridesmaid of the 1920s: "The tall champion took just one look at this hurrying storm cloud and proceeded to serve four aces with such terrific speed and control that even the brilliant Johnston was forced to stand helpless."[3]

A player of such skill and dominance as Tilden would seem to have needed no defenders. Yet that is what Rice became for Big Bill, the tennis player he considered far and away the best in history. Like Rice, everyone marveled at Tilden's tennis. Yet when critics raised questions about artificial drama in his matches, and when the U.S. Lawn Tennis Association made trouble for Tilden in the 1920s, it was Rice who came to the star's defense. Tilden's troubles off the court later in life also found Rice ready to help and to explain, even though Tilden's actions offended Rice's sensibilities.

"Of all the changes in the world of sports that took place between the years 1920 and 1930 none was more astonishing or unpredictable than the emergence of lawn tennis as a spectator game and prime box-office attraction," Paul Gallico has written.[4] Tilden's first U.S. singles championship in 1920 marked the end of the social age of tennis and the beginning of the period when tennis players took their places in the public eye alongside other sports celebrities. With Rice marveling at Tilden's power and quickness, tennis developed a new image of athleticism. Sportswriters turned Tilden's often dramatic net exploits into dramatic newspaper copy. The United States championships at Forest Hills and the Davis Cup matches gained status as major events as the nation followed Tilden's title quests. In the public mind, Tilden became tennis.[5]

Although Tilden had won the U.S. mixed-doubles championship with Mary K. Browne in 1913, he lost in the finals of the national singles championship in 1918 and 1919 and did not win that prestigious title until 1920, when he was twenty-seven years old. Tilden did not lose again in singles play at Forest Hills and Wimbledon or in the Davis Cup until 1926. He helped the United States win the Davis Cup seven consecutive years, added the 1929 U.S. singles title to the six he won from 1920 to 1925 as well as five U.S. doubles championships, and won Wimbledon three times.

Bill Tilden

Tilden was so dominating that he once won fifty-seven straight games.[6] Rice wrote in 1924 that Tilden, even more than the home run–hitting Ruth, "comes extremely close to being our dominant crown wearer, the one champion who outclasses his field by a wider margin than anyone else." In a profile of Tilden for *Collier's*, Rice told a story to illustrate Tilden's dominance. At the end of a losing set, a friend told Tilden that he had made a ten-dollar bet that Tilden would win the next set 6-2. Rice reported that Tilden replied, "All right, we'll make it 6-2," then won the set by that score. "He is one of the few who can ride along easily and then rise suddenly to great heights at any given moment that may suit his whim," Rice concluded.[7] Others noted the same thing about Tilden. And they wondered why, if he could knock four aces past Bill Johnston to avoid a thunderstorm or win by a particular score at will, he so often teetered on the edge of defeat before rallying to snatch away victory with an uncanny exhibition of skill and fortitude. It was generally accepted by tennis observers of the time that Tilden did this on purpose.

Tilden so dominated tennis during his heyday that he was always the overwhelming favorite to win every match. Yet crowds seldom were rooting for the underdog at the end of a match, as Tilden often came scrambling out of a deep hole with a furious onslaught. Tilden, who wanted to be a stage actor, seemed just that on the court, because of his showman's flair for the dramatic. He captured the emotions of his fans. He remained a popular favorite in spite of his continuous victories and his temperamental court scenes.[8]

More recent bad boys of tennis, such as Illie Nastase, Jimmy Connors, and John McEnroe, introduced little new to the sport in the area of petulance. At times Tilden would obviously throw points to show contempt for a linesman's call that he felt had erroneously gone in his favor.[9] Although he refused to accept an advantage he had not earned, he could be hard on officials who went against him. John R. Tunis, the tennis writer for the *New*

Yorker and the *New York Evening Post* during Tilden's time, described the star's court behavior in this way: "He will turn and glare at any lineman who dares give a decision against his judgment; before the thousands in the stands he will demand the removal of the offender; he will request 'lets' at crucial moments, object when new balls are thrown out."[10] When he mis-hit a shot, Tilden would stand with his hands on his hips and exclaim, "Oh, Peaches!" Al Laney, a colleague of Rice in New York sports writing, wrote in Tilden's obituary that the tennis star was "arrogant, quarrelsome, unreasonable; very hard to get along with."[11] Even Rice noted that Tilden was "a nervous, restless type, inclined to petulancy when he doesn't like certain decisions."

Rice, however, did not agree that Tilden scripted his dramatic victories. Instead, he portrayed Tilden as a player who always rose to the challenge. On too many occasions, Rice had seen Tilden pull out a victory after being only one point from defeat. In 1925, Rice wrote: "It has been said that Tilden takes it easy and draws the line to a fine edge before he really bounds forward with his best. This may be true on many occasions. But no man is going to draw a line so thin and fine that only a single point stands between him and defeat. That's crowding it a bit. It is under the heaviest pressure, in the toughest spot, against the longest odds that Tilden is at his best. He simply won't be trimmed."[12]

Rice thought there was no athlete with his back against the wall quite so hard to beat as Tilden. He credited Tilden's ability to rally when nearly beaten to a "reserve force, which left him something to work on when the storm clouds arrived." Rice recalled seeing one match in which "Tilden was out on the edge of barren lands, ready to disappear into the mists." Trailing his opponent two sets to none, Tilden called on his reserve force, and "he crashed through to victory with a game no one could hold in check."[13]

Tilden had much more going for him than just a reserve force. Rice took many opportunities to marvel at the tennis player during the first half of the 1920s. Rice's remarks served to reinforce the aura of invincibility that surrounded Tilden. Rice thought Tilden had the physical qualifications needed for tennis stardom, being "somewhat lighter on his feet than a cat or a leopard"[14] as well as having "the greatest pair of legs in sport, coupled with unbelievable stamina."[15] Rice also saw in Tilden the same purposefulness of thought that he noted in some of the other sports stars of the period:

> Did you ever watch the expressions on the faces of such competitors as Jack Dempsey, Walter Hagen, Ty Cobb, Babe Ruth or Bill Tilden in action? If you have you will have noticed about each an atmosphere of concentration, concentration upon a certain program which they have mapped out with no waste of thought upon any outside factors.
>
> They are merely thinking through the job at hand—all the way through to the finish of the act.
>
> Form, speed, power, skill and strength are of course highly important ingredients in building competitive success. But they are not the entire story. There must be a mental force back of these qualities which in the main consists of determination and concentration, two elements which can crash through a concrete wall.[16]

All these factors, Rice wrote, came together to make Tilden the perfect tennis player, a man who, in 1924, seemingly could not lose: "Tilden has combined all the needed physical assets with hard training and with constant thought and study of his game. He has taken nothing for granted about his skill; and in this he has learned one of the most important rules in sport. . . . He is one of the few invincible figures of sport."[17]

On September 11, 1926, Rene Lacoste defeated Tilden 4-6, 6-4, 8-6, 8-6 in a match in the Davis Cup final round between France and the United States. Tilden, who had not lost a major singles match since 1919, lost again less than a week later in the quarterfinal round of the U.S. championship. Again he lost to a French player, as Henri Cochet took a 6-8, 6-1, 6-3, 1-6, 8-6 victory, Tilden's reserve force apparently failing him in the deciding set. Unknown to almost anyone, Tilden had torn cartilage in his knee during the loss to Lacoste but had played out the meaningless final match of the United States' Davis Cup victory rather than default.[18] Fred Hawthorne, the tennis writer for the *New York Herald-Tribune* at the time, reported, "Big Bill has reigned with a despotism so absolute during the last six years that it was difficult for that gallery to conceive of his actually being beaten and his title wrested away from him."[19]

Lacoste won the U.S. championship that year. A week later, Rice was busy assessing Tilden's chances of regaining "his" championship. Rice noted that the next time the title would be contested at Forest Hills, Tilden would be thirty-four, ten years older than Lacoste. The odds would be against him, Rice wrote, "yet the power and genius of a Tilden are not to be thrown into the discard with any idle gesture."[20] Rice counted on Tilden to rise to the challenge as he had for the previous six years. He had confidence in the determination of a player who could not make the top six on the University of Pennsylvania tennis team in 1913 but ranked as the number-one player in the United States from 1920 to 1929.[21]

In May, Rice told the readers of *Collier's* that Tilden's eagerness to regain his lost titles was so great that Tilden would not wait for the French to come to the United States but was going to France and Wimbledon to play.[22] In his newspaper column in August, Rice continued to gasp at Tilden's pace and wondered if he could keep it up through the Davis Cup and U.S. championships in September. "If he can he will be one of the most remarkable competitive products ever known," Rice wrote.[23]

Even though Tilden had lost to Lacoste in the Davis Cup final in 1926, the United States defeated France. The United States had won the Davis Cup for seven consecutive years, winning in the finals four times by 5-0 scores and three times by 4-1 marks. Yet the French team—Lacoste, Cochet, Jean Borota, and Jacques Brugnon, nicknamed the Four Musketeers—seemed the team to beat in 1927. Rice quoted Tilden on the United States' chances: "We are not licked yet. If hard work and harder fighting counts, we still have a chance against the best flock of young tennis stars any nation ever sent to the game at one time."[24]

The statement was full of heroic intentions, like so many of the quotes that infrequently appeared in Rice's stories. But Tilden's intentions did not quite match his play, and his comeback fell short. He lost to Lacoste in the U.S. national championship match and in a Davis Cup singles match. As Tilden left the court after the Davis Cup defeat, the stunned crowd of 15,186 at the Germantown Cricket Club, Tilden's home court, rose in a standing ovation. Some of the spectators were crying. With Little Bill Johnston at the end of his playing career and almost sure to lose his matches, the French team had planned to use its strong quartet to wear down Tilden, a thirty-four-year-old with a bad knee. The strategy worked. Tilden won in the opening singles match and in the doubles match, but lost to Lacoste 6-3, 4-6, 6-3, 6-2. France won the Davis Cup 3-2.[25] France also beat the United States in the finals in 1928, 1929, and 1930, as it won the Davis Cup for six consecutive years. The United States did not win the Davis Cup again until 1937.

Although Rice continued to express confidence in Tilden when his tenure at the top ended, U.S. Lawn Tennis Association (USLTA) officials saw the end of Tilden's invincibility as an opening to discipline the troublesome star. Before he became the personification of tennis, Tilden had covered theater and sports for the *Philadelphia Public Ledger*. After he became the nation's tennis champion, Tilden received as much as twenty-five thousand dollars a year to write tennis columns for the paper's syndicate. In 1924, the USLTA told Tilden this practice violated its amateur code. Tilden ignored the threat of suspension, but the association took no disciplinary action. The USLTA needed him as its biggest draw and the best player on the Davis Cup team.[26] Later that year, Rice and Tilden served on a committee to study the dispute over amateurism and bylines. The committee reached a compromise that allowed amateur players to write professionally as long as they did not cover an event in which they were participating.

With Tilden in Europe and the 1928 Davis Cup final less than a month away, the executive committee of the USLTA suspended Tilden from amateur tennis because of his writing income. With the French team seemingly as unbeatable as Tilden had once been, the USLTA officials took the opportunity to take down Tilden. But their action sparked an international furor. The French had built a stadium at Roland Garros as a showplace for their people to see the Musketeers meet Tilden in France's first defense of its Davis Cup title. The French government contacted the United States government, and under directions from President Coolidge, Myron Herrick, the U.S. ambassador to France, got the suspension lifted. The decision was not announced until the day before Davis Cup play was to start. Tilden, who had spent most of his time in France playing bridge because he did think he would be allowed to participate in the Davis Cup matches, defeated Lacoste in five sets in their singles match.[27]

Rice criticized the USLTA for singling out Tilden for disciplinary action. He urged the association to drop its hypocritical amateur rules and allow professionals to play in its tournaments. He wrote in his column during the furor surrounding Tilden's suspension: "Barring Tilden and letting conditions remain as they are will mean little or nothing. The sanest way out would be to forget the player-writer rule entirely. As conditions have now developed it might be just as well to forget the amateur side and have open tournaments."[28]

Tilden turned professional in 1931, after winning the singles championships at Forest Hills in 1929 and Wimbledon in 1930. For years Tilden was the main attraction on a barnstorming circuit of pro tennis. He played professionally until he was fifty-nine years old. Rice wrote that even at that age for one set Tilden remained the best player in the world.[29]

But Tilden had an unhappy and troubled life after the Golden Age. If any of the sportswriters knew Tilden was a homosexual while he stood astride world tennis, the knowledge never appeared in their newspapers. Homosexuality was a taboo subject for the newspapers. Tilden seemed to have few, if any, sexual contacts of any kind while he was the world's best tennis player. But after he turned professional, he started traveling with adolescent male companions. In 1946, Tilden was charged with contributing to the delinquency of a minor after Los Angeles police observed his actions and then stopped his car, which was being driven by a fourteen-year-old boy. Rather than this misdemeanor charge, Tilden could have been charged with a felony, lewd and lascivious behavior with a minor. Rice wrote one of fifteen letters of reference to the court on behalf of Tilden, who nonetheless served seven and a half months of a one-year jail sentence.[30]

Rice devoted a chapter to Tilden in his autobiography, which was published less than two years after Tilden's death and about a month after his own. In his remembrances of Tilden, Rice did not mention homosexuality or Tilden's arrest. He recalled the many times in the Golden Age he referred to Tilden as an artist on the court. He wrote that Tilden was "a tragic artist at the end" and that "tennis was one-hundred percent Bill's life—whenever he strayed from the court he was pathetic." The closest Rice came to the topic was to offer a bit of amateur psychology on Tilden's problems after the glory days. Rice reported that Tilden had been babied as a child by his mother, had spent most of his formative years under the guardianship of women, and had received girlish gifts at Christmas. "I'm convinced that his abnormal upbringing gave him a complex," Rice concluded.[31] It was a last attempt by Rice at a defense for the player he considered the greatest in tennis history and whom he wished to remember and to have remembered as possessing the sterling qualities of a champion athlete, as "a tennis player of brains, generalship, speed, power and amazing skill"[32] rather than a near-penniless man on the fringes of society.

Tilden won his last major championship in 1930 at Wimbledon at the age of thirty-seven. Forty-four years later, when Ken Rosewall reached the Wimbledon championship match at the age of forty, a reporter pointed out to him that he could supplant Tilden as the oldest champion in the tournament's history. In reply, Rosewall shook his head slightly and said quietly, "Ah, but that was Tilden."[33]

CHAPTER 7

Red Grange

Sports in the 1920s featured a parade of nicknames. Sportswriters called tennis star Helen Wills, Little Miss Poker Face; Jack Dempsey, the Manassa Mauler; and Luis Angel Firpo, the Wild Bull of the Pampas. Babe wasn't enough of a nickname for George Herman Ruth, so he became the Bambino and the Sultan of Swat. Notre Dame's backfield gained fame as the Four Horsemen, and the crooked members of the 1919 Chicago White Sox gained notoriety as the Black Sox. It was always Big Bill Tilden and Little Bill Johnston. The strong tennis quartet from France became the Four Musketeers. Even Bobby Jones's putter had a nickname, Calamity Jane. The decade itself had nicknames—the Golden Age, Roaring Twenties, Dry Decade, Era of Excess, Era of Wonderful Nonsense, Jazz Age.[1]

But of all the nicknames of the time, Grantland Rice's nickname for Red Grange, the Galloping Ghost, seemed the closest to perfection. In two words Rice captured the image of Grange at his best and imparted it to millions who would never attend a University of Illinois football game. In the newsreels of the day, with tacklers seeming to pass through his flickering image, Grange probably appeared as wraithlike as a living human could.[2]

Rice tried other nicknames on Grange. In a two-page story for *Collier's* in 1924, Rice pinned six appellations on Grange without once using the Galloping Ghost—the flaming meteor of Illinois, the flying terror, a new knight of the elusive foot, this phenomenon of the plains, the Will o' the Wisp, and a human tornado.[3]

But the spectral image of the ghost—an untouchable ballcarrier—
occurs regularly in Rice's work on Grange. When Grange broke
loose on a long run, he seemed supernatural to Rice. Near the
end of his last collegiate game, Grange returned an interception
forty-two yards. Rice described the run as though Grange had
been loosed from hell for a dusk haunting: "They were looking
upon the final sprint of the Galloping Ghost, including all the
adjectives you can think of or find in the dictionary. . . . There
were deep shadows on the field now, but No. 77 still flamed as
he crossed one chalk mark after another. . . . And the 85,000 were
satisfied at last. They had seen the ghost, the phantom, the spec-
ter, or what you will, gallop lightly over fast turf for nearly half
a length of the field."[4]

Rice wrote perhaps more verse about Grange than about any
other individual athlete, and ghost imagery was a prominent
part of these poems. Rice's best verse on an athlete might be this
one, written after Grange's first appearance in New York as a
professional player:

> There are two shapes now moving,
> Two ghosts that drift and glide,
> And which of them to tackle
> Each rival must decide;
> They shift with spectral swiftness
> Across the swarded range,
> And one of them's a shadow,
> And one of them is Grange.[5]

Walter Camp, the former Yale coach who began picking All-
America teams in 1889, selected Grange as a back on his 1923 All-
America squad. Grange led Illinois through an undefeated season as a sophomore, but even Camp's recognition did not make
much of an impression in the Northeast, which still served as the
focal point of collegiate football. Although already an All-American, Grange hit the national scene in one game—a 1924 contest

Red Grange

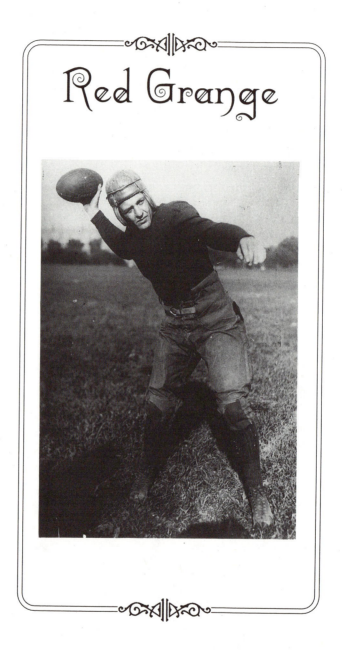

with Michigan. Rice called Grange's performance in the game "the greatest single exhibition ever known upon a football field."

Michigan had not lost in twenty games when it visited Illinois's new stadium. Grange returned the opening kickoff ninety-five yards for a touchdown. "On the first play, Grange took the kick-off and ran through those eleven Michigan tacklers with a display of speed and a baffling dodging ability that no man has ever seen matched," Rice wrote of Grange's touchdown return.[6] Grange then scored on runs of 67, 56, and 45 yards on his first 3 rushes from scrimmage. Illinois won 39-14, the most points scored against Michigan since the turn of the century. Grange rushed fifteen times for 212 yards and 4 touchdowns, completed 6 of 8 passes for 64 yards and a touchdown, and returned 3 kickoffs for 126 yards and a touchdown.[7] The performance inspired Rice's first verse on Grange:

> A streak of fire, a breath of flame,
> Eluding all who reach and clutch;
> A gray ghost thrown into the game
> That rival hands may rarely touch.[8]

The game marked the beginning of what came to be called the "Grange ballyhoo." Week after week throughout the season, newspapers and their readers watched to see what new feats the five-foot, ten-inch tall, 170-pound junior with the orange seventy-seven on his blue jersey would accomplish. Grange earned All-America recognition again and entered the 1925 season as the most heralded player in the nation. But a combination of stacked defenses, a position change to quarterback, and mud-soaked fields kept the Illinois star from performing as flamboyantly as he had in the 1924 season. Some All-America team selectors left Grange off their squads. Rice, who had taken over the Walter Camp selections for *Collier's*, included Grange on his all-star team, the country's most respected. After the season, Rice used his newspaper column to argue with Grange's detractors:

There still are many marveling at the size of the Grange ballyhoo.
They argue that he didn't have as good a season as Oberlander,
Wilson, Tryon or Nevers. They are right. But he had a good two-
year jump on that bunch and his fall program was built for drama.
He got off to a slow start. Then he bounded back against Butler
and Iowa. He flopped again against Michigan. . . . And then just
as the anvil chorus was about to resound merrily and noisily once
more he lifted the cheering nation to its feet against Pennsylvania.
. . . That was the afternoon that made Red Grange in 1925. . . . That
was the game that proved again the speed of his feet and the cun-
ning of his varying pace.[9]

Grange made his only collegiate appearance outside the Midwest when Illinois visited Pennsylvania in 1925. The game became Grange's second foundation for fame, proving to skeptics
and backsliders that the 1924 performance had not been a fluke
and giving substance to the hyperbole in Rice's praise and poetry of the Galloping Ghost.

On a field with mud ankle deep in some places, Grange led Illinois to a 24-2 victory over the previously unbeaten Quakers. Grange
scored on touchdown runs of 56, 13, and 20 yards as he gained 237
yards on 28 carries and added another 126 yards on reception and
kick returns.[10] Rice called Grange "the Orange Phantom who turned
mud and water into a cinder track for flying feet" and went on at
length about the performance in his wrap-up of the weekend's
college football for the *New York Herald-Tribune:*

> This Red Grange performance, under the conditions, must remain as
> one of the most remarkable of all achievements written in football's
> book. . . . After a tough year, Fate gave the willowy Westerner with
> the spiral hips an unbeaten team to face upon a quagmire, and he
> ran its tongue into the mud and mire.
>
> Out of the big whirl the great figure of the afternoon was a
> dancing Dervish in an orange helmet, a greyhound where the

ground was dry, an eel where the water blocked his way. There were 11 men, all famous football players, who had been given one main assignment, and that was to stop Grange. But when Grange gets started 11 are not enough. There should be something in the rules to let an opponent subpoena three full squads when the redhead reaches the open.

These three squads can get a lot of useful exercise chasing him across the goal line. They run some backs out of bounds beyond the sideline. They run Grange out of bounds back of the goal posts.[11]

Grange seemed as much an All-American off the field as on it. He didn't date until he reached college. He was a solid student and played basketball and baseball at Illinois. He neither drank nor smoked.[12] (After turning pro, Grange had the chance to endorse a brand of cigarettes, but he told his business manager he couldn't because he didn't smoke. The manager told Grange he would only have to say he liked the cigarettes' aroma.) Grange also had an outrageous sense of modesty. He maintained that his biggest football thrill came in 1923 when he held the ball for a forty-seven-yard field goal kicked by Earl Britton in a 9-6 victory over Iowa. Iowa had not lost since the 1920 season. Grange never mentioned that he scored the winning touchdown in that game with two minutes left to play.[13]

Two days after Grange's final college game, Rice wrote that Grange had the complete respect of every opposing team and player. "This is more important than his long runs, but it will not be remembered as long."[14] Rice and other sports writers helped assure that Grange would endure in memory as a football idol rather than as a swell guy by writing considerably more about Grange's ball-carrying ability than his sterling character. Rice himself was intrigued particularly by the grace and smoothness of Grange in the open field. He described Grange's running style for a *Collier's* article in 1924: "There is no gathering of muscles for an extra lunge. There is only the effortless, ghost-like weave and glide upon effortless legs with a body that can detach itself from the hips—with a change of pace that can come to a dead stop and pick up instant speed, so perfect is the coordination of brain and sinew. There has been no running back in football history who had these baffling, bewildering qualities to such an extent."[15]

Although he often transformed Grange into an untouchable ghost in his writing, Rice could detach himself from romantic allusions to comprehend the physical punishment Grange took as a star running back. Rice lauded Grange's determination and durability, but the ghost imagery crept into even such practical praise, as from a 1925 *Collier's* article titled "The Stuff Men Are Made Of": "Any time Red Grange can discover a spot upon his body that isn't black or blue he should give three rousing cheers. The star must pay his penalty. He is watched more closely and is tackled with just a trifle more intensity. Rival teams watch every move Grange makes, paying him therefore the finest of tributes. They know that, once in the open, his speed, his general elusiveness and his baffling change of pace turn him into a phantom beyond the reach of human hands."[16]

Grange's down-to-earth attributes helped make him an out-of-this-world football player. His knack for breaking loose on game-winning touchdown runs thrilled Rice, who had the ability to pass along his excitement to readers: "If there had been time left, concentration and determination might have hammered the ball in steady advances up the field. But seconds here were vital. They were as important as years. And in that great moment, battered, half-broken, weary and about spent, Red Grange suddenly became more than merely human as he eluded every Maroon tackler and ran more than 80 yards to Chicago's goal."[17]

Performances such as that propelled Grange into the public consciousness. By 1925, Rice was describing as "Grange-like" long runs made by other backs.[18] In profiling the members of the *Collier's* 1925 All-America team, Rice wrote Grange "had greater magnetism and greater personality than any member of football's 60-year parade."[19] Attendance at Illinois games jumped in the 1925 season to 371,000, after only 182,000 spectators saw the Illini home games in 1924.[20] In November, Chicago admirers circulated a petition to put Grange's name on the ballot as a candidate for the Republican nomination for congressman-at-large in a primary election.[21] When the Chicago Bears beat the Giants in Grange's pro debut in New York in December, the headline of the front-page story in the *New York Herald-Tribune* read "70,000 See Grange Win, 19-7."[22]

Bob Zuppke, the innovative football coach for whom Grange played at Illinois, once said, "Often an All-American is made by a long run, a weak defense, and a poet in the press box."[23] All of those things might have helped make Grange famous, but Rice explained Grange's popularity in football terms: "The broken-field runner, the ground-gainer in football, has always carried an appeal to packed stands beyond any other factor of the game."[24] Rice described this appeal in his report on Grange's final collegiate game: "There was a thrill every moment Grange was in the game. There was a lack of thrill when he left it for the third period. He was fully as much personality as he was speed and running strength. It was not only what he did, but what he might do, at any moment."

Grange's many long touchdown runs had made it possible to believe he could score on any play, Rice explained in his column one day later: "Grange, more than all, was a threat. When Grange took the ball there was always the feeling that each run might be a touchdown. His great gift lay where the crowd could see. And the crowd could see not only unusual skill beyond the line of scrimmage but also unusual symmetry and rhythm, judgment and speed."[25]

Even at the time, Rice wrote of Grange in the past tense. Rice had every reason to believe that Grange's football career had ended, or at the very least, had ended for that season, when he saw Illinois beat Ohio State 14-9 to cap the collegiate season. The game seemed a fine finale for Grange as a collegiate-record crowd of 85,000 spectators attended in Columbus, Ohio. Grange rushed for 113 yards in the game and made two interceptions in the last two minutes. When Rice reported the game, Grange was the only player he mentioned in the first 817 words of his story. Rice was aware that Grange had been considering offers to join the National Football League, which was then in its seventh year. Rice described Grange as "playing under a smashing nerve strain, where for over a week, he had been the most worried and the most harried athlete in the country."[26] Grange signed a contract to play for the Chicago Bears following the game and made his professional debut five days later on Thanksgiving Day in a game against the Chicago Cardinals.

The game at Wrigley Field drew the first sellout crowd in Bears' history, thirty-six thousand spectators at a time when the team considered five thousand an outstanding turnout. The publicity and excitement Grange brought to professional football stood as the greatest single influence on the game until television made its impact.[27] The immediate reaction, though, was not over Grange's impact on pro football, but pro football's impact on Grange. The public debate over Grange's decision to go into professional football included those who felt Grange had acted unethically by capitalizing on his college reputation for personal gain. To these critics, his flight from college seemed to shatter the image of the gentleman-scholar who played for the joy of the game and the honor of the school.[28]

Rice always preferred college football to the professional variety, but he saw nothing wrong with playing football for money. "There is nothing illegal or unmoral or unethical about pro football when it is conducted in the right way," Rice wrote for *Collier's,* leaving the impression that the current state of the NFL might not have been that right way.[29] Soon after his signing, many sportswriters came to Grange's defense, writing that he was "an innocent, decent, trusting chap" who was the "victim of a kind of conspiracy of get-rich-quick promoters who did not care how far they went in prostituting him to their ends." But Grange bluntly defused these apologists by saying he saw no reason not to accept the professional money and profit from his ability as soon as he could.[30]

Rice proved to be more of a realist than his colleagues in evaluating the situation. As he often did with Grange, he used a short verse:

> When Harold Grange, the gay young kid,
> Blew off his amateur lid,
> Most college folk cried out "For Shame"—
> But marveled at him just the same.
> And he was slick and he was wise
> To thus jump in and advertise.[31]

On the day of Grange's pro debut, Rice wrote in his column that becoming a professional player probably was the wise choice for Grange, who could expect a quick and large reward. But for almost all other college players, Rice thought it would be better for them to complete their educations and move into some other endeavor than to join the pro league and in three or four years find themselves without a job or savings.[32]

In his year-end wrap-up for the *New York Herald-Tribune,* Rice noted that Grange's arrival had boosted the NFL to major-league status in the public mind, adding that only greed could wreck the progress made by Grange's month in the league: "As a result of this publicity the pro game got a big start, and if correctly directed it will be no small feature of next season's program. Professional football has come to stay unless it is badly mishandled, and this is exactly what happened when C. C. Pyle, Grange's manager, arranged one of those 'for revenue only' schedules, which crippled Grange, wore out the rest of the team and punctured a lot of early interest."[33]

Grange suffered an arm injury during the Bears' exhaustive schedule and missed a week of play. But neither that injury nor Rice's warning kept C. C. Pyle, who had been given the nickname Cash-and-Carry, and the Bears from undertaking a tour of the South and West to capitalize on Grange's fame. After an eight-day layoff, the Bears played nine more games between Christmas Day and January 31, giving the team a total of nineteen games in seventeen cities in the sixty-six days after Grange joined the club. No tour by a sports team had ever received so much publicity or proved so profitable. But Grange could not take the pounding such a schedule entailed, and his production could not keep pace with his press clippings.[34]

Rice seemed disappointed not so much with Grange's inability to flash his old form as with Grange allowing himself to be put in a position where he could not do his best:

> [Grange] also had dreams of the super-heroic. He was either kidding himself or kidding the public when he tried to play seven or eight games in 10 days.
>
> From a near superman Grange turned into a second-class back before the first two weeks of his pro career were over.
>
> In two or three games he was the worst back on the field, too worn out to play any game.
>
> He permitted Pyle to use him as a decoy to lure out crowds who came out to see a star, and saw only a weary, bedraggled athlete trying to gain a yard now and then or keep from losing more than two or three. No near superman ever flopped at greater speed.[35]

In 1927, Grange suffered a knee injury and did not play for a season and a half. When he returned to football, he had lost his elusive running ability—the ghost was gone. Grange played for the Bears from 1929 to 1934, serving as a good blocking and receiving halfback and an outstanding defensive back. He made the

NFL all-star team in 1931, but he did so without the dazzling skill in the open field he had before his injury.[36]

In the November 22, 1924, issue of *Collier's*, Rice wrote an article about the best football players he had seen and tabbed Eddie Mahan, who played for Harvard from 1913 to 1915, as the best broken-field runner in football history.[37] Less than a month later, in another article in *Collier's*, Rice had promoted Grange to that honor[38] and started his long struggle over Grange's place in football history.

When Rice saw Grange perform as the Galloping Ghost image, his immediate writings would proclaim him as the best running back in football history. Less than a week after Grange's big game against Pennsylvania, Rice wrote: "He is a will-o'-the-wisp built of steel. There is nothing brittle in the make-up of this human miracle who has been marked for slaughter for three years in a row. There never has been a greater ball carrier in football history than Grange."[39] Yet in his column the day after Grange's final collegiate game, Rice wrote that Grange's football skills did not equal those of some of the sport's greats. Several players whose names are known now only to ardent football historians were deemed by Rice to have been better than Grange:

> As an all-around star upon both offense and defense, Grange was not up to the standards set by Jim Thorpe, George Gipp, Willie Heston, Ned Mahan, Swede Oberlander, Eddie Tryon, George Wilson or Ernie Nevers, to mention a few.
>
> But Grange, in addition to his ball-carrying skill, has grace, rhythm and personality. He was a quiet young man upon the gridiron or around the campus, yet he had the vital spark. He was proof that one doesn't have to manufacture the flame by lighting many bonfires. He was proof that one cannot manufacture the flame in this way. He had it within himself. . . . He will not be remembered as the greatest of all, but he will have his place among the gridiron immortals.[40]

Less than a week later, Rice wrote: "Grange remains as great a ballcarrier as ever played—beyond the scrimmage line. But not the greatest of all stars. He isn't a Gipp, a Thorpe, a Heston. Perhaps it is quite enough now to be a Grange."[41] But a week after that, Rice used his column to interview Grange's college coach, who attested to Grange's skills as more than just a ballcarrier, but as a top-flight, all-around player skilled in blocking, tackling, and passing.[42] Writing with what seemed like exasperation a few weeks later in an aside in his column to "R. H. K.," Rice said, "For at least the tenth time we repeat—Grange in college was the greatest running back, the greatest ball carrier we have ever seen. He was more than a great broken field runner—he helped to break up the fields."[43]

Rice asked Grange to help him select an all-time all-star football team for inclusion in his autobiography in 1954. Grange, typically, suggested he did not belong on such a squad. Rice included him anyway, along with Jim Thorpe and Bronko Nagurski as the greatest running backs to play both professional and college football.[44] The Football Writers Association of America selected an all-time all-star team in 1969 to celebrate college football's centennial. Forty-four years after the end of his collegiate career, Grange was the only unanimous choice on the modern (1919 to 1969) all-star team selected by the FWAA.[45]

Commenting on his fame in 1926, Grange said, "Ten years from now, no one will know or care what Red Grange did or who he was."[46] A few months earlier, Rice had written, "Red will soon be a myth, a romantic ghost from forgotten years."[47] Grange, of course, was wrong, and Rice, the mythmaker who transformed a football player into an immortal ghost, was correct.

CHAPTER 8

Knute Rockne

After Notre Dame beat West Virginia in the Fiesta Bowl to claim
the college football national championship for the 1988 season,
reports on the game invariably recalled "the legendary Knute
Rockne" and the six national championships won by his teams
at Notre Dame. One reporter noted that a cloud formation above
Sun Devil Stadium resembled Rockne's visage. That must have
been a rather strange group of clouds, because Westbrook Pegler
once wrote of Rockne, "He looks like the old punched-up pre-
liminary fighter who becomes a door-tender in a speakeasy and
sits at a shadowy table in the corner near the door at night, re-
calling the time he fought Billy Papke in Peoria for fifty dollars."[1]

Sixty years after his death, Rockne seems as much a character of legend as King Arthur. Fiction and exaggeration entwined
around the core of the Rockne story from its beginning. The lore
of Rockne combined with his personality and accomplishments
to create a folk hero. Grantland Rice helped. Certainly, Rice shaped
portions of this lore. His stories about Rockne and Rockne's teams
became embedded in the national consciousness.

Rockne has been called college football's prophet and Rice
college football's friend.[2] Both made contributions to the rapid
growth of the game during the 1920s. Between 1921 and 1930,
attendance at college football games doubled and gate receipts
tripled.[3] No team enjoyed a more spectacular attendance increase
than Rockne's at Notre Dame. In Rockne's third season as head

coach, only 85,000 spectators attended Notre Dame games. Three years later, in 1923, the number had grown to 197,000. In 1926, it was up to 350,000. By 1928, 419,705 spectators saw the Irish play, even though Notre Dame's home field held only 27,000 fans. In 1929, while a new Notre Dame stadium was being built, the Irish played all their games on the road. In that year, 551,112 spectators saw the Notre Dame games.

The games between Notre Dame and the United States Military Academy symbolized, more than other contests, the change in football during this period. The classic encounters between the Irish and the Cadets lifted college football from a regional focus accented by Northeastern snobbery to an intersectional mania. From 1919 to 1923, only seventy thousand spectators attended the five Notre Dame–Army games.[4] Following the now legendary Notre Dame–Army game of 1924, when Rice wrote his famous Four Horsemen story, the single-game crowds exceeded that five-year turnout for the rest of the decade. Sportswriter Red Smith wrote that Rice made the Notre Dame–Army game a big event.[5] This rivalry not only spawned the Four Horsemen but also featured the Gipper, and in 1920, this was where Rice and Rockne met.

Not surprisingly, they became friends, bonded by their idealistic outlook toward their favorite sport. Rice summarized those feelings in a column in 1925 when he wrote: "What in the first place, are the qualities which football calls for? Condition, courage, stamina, loyalty, service, team play, fortitude and skill. There are no finer qualities in any line of existence. There has been no finer game yet devised for the youth of any country."[6] Spirit and tradition formed the foundation for Rice's joy in college football. Rockne and his teams seemed steeped in both. Upon Rockne's death in 1931, Rice wrote, "In his career at Notre Dame, Knute Rockne had built up a spirit beyond anything football has ever known. His amazing personality reached every part of the campus."[7]

Considered a peerless manipulator of his players' emotions, Rockne had practical as well as romantic reasons for emphasiz-

Knute Rockne

ing spirit and tradition. In his handbook on football coaching, Rockne wrote of the value of tradition: "The history or traditions of the school are a great thing to recite to your team, and to keep before them. Exaggerate these as much as you can, and set a somewhat exaggerated standard to emulate. A school without traditions will find it very hard to build a successful football team, as tradition is a powerful factor."[8]

Not everyone shared Rice and Rockne's romanticized view of football. As college football exploded into national prominence, critics charged the game had overstepped its purpose at institutions of higher learning. Nebraska halfback Bud McBride said college players were "just monkeys in a circus," and Jefferson S. Burrus, Jr., of Wisconsin charged in his pamphlet "The Present Intercollegiate Athletic System" that colleges exploited players as though they were fighting cocks.[9] Newspapers were accused of creating a monster. In 1926 an article in the *Independent* titled "Football— Overgrown Darling of the Press" noted:

> The grotesque overgrowth of the game is apparent. It is much commented upon, but the doctors can't agree on who fed the fair-haired boy so much fattening candy. The papers say, "We give the public what it wants. Did not 300,000 people witness eight football games on Oct. 16, with the season just hitting its stride?" But asks the skeptic, how many would have gone to see New York University and Tulane play, how many would have attended the Notre Dame–Penn State contest, if newspapers all over the country had not been heralding Tulane and Notre Dame as the greatest peripatetic football teams on record? Would Tulane have traveled 4,000 miles in three weeks if the papers had not assured the gate receipts?[10]

Rice and Rockne spoke out against the movement to deemphasize college football; Rice wrote of the virtues involved in the game,

and Rockne met with educators to expound on the same message. But even as a personification of the idealized view of college
football, Rockne kept his practical side. He supervised almost every
detail in the construction of Notre Dame's new stadium, paying
particular attention to providing the press with first-class accom-
modations.[11]

Throughout his career Rice decried the winning-at-any-cost attitude he thought afflicted college football, holding that "a coach that
isn't building character should be fired." In his autobiography, Rice
held up Rockne and Notre Dame as examples of what should be
preserved while the hypocrisy and dirt were cleaned away: "Did
you ever hear of any scandal connected with Knute Rockne and
the Four Horsemen? With Red Grange, the Galloping Ghost? I will
stand for the fierce and continued spirit of Notre Dame teams. They
have led the list through the years. Spirit is the most vital of all football factors. They got this from the Fathers at Notre Dame and from
Knute Rockne. It can't and should not be destroyed."[12]

Rockne's winning character accompanied a keen football mind.
"There have been football coaches as great as Rockne was . . . but,
like Ruth and Dempsey, Knute Rockne had a personality no other
football coach has ever reached," Rice wrote.[13] But he also called
Rockne "the master instructor"[14] and "the man who put more
beauty and speed and skill into football than any coach that ever
lived."[15] In a column that appeared following news that Rockne had
signed a contract to coach at Columbia, Rice clearly expresses his
view of Rockne's coaching ability. Rockne changed his mind about
leaving Notre Dame but not before Rice had written:

> Knute Rockne's arrival at Columbia is one of the most important
> coaching moves in the history of the game. Rockne has been so
> much of Notre Dame football that the two names have always
> traveled together. He is undoubtedly one of the coaching geniuses
> of all times, not only a great teacher, but also a great builder who

happens to be a master at every department of the game. He is one
of the great morale makers, and that is a feature of football coaching
that has never received its just due. Columbia, under Rockne, will be
one of the most formidable opponents in the game. . . . He will have
the Lion of the Hudson roaring before next fall is over.[16]

If being a morale maker had never received its just due previously, then Rockne made up for past neglect, as it became his
most enduring legacy. "He had an infectious magnetism that
went into the hearts and souls of his men. He carried the brand
of inspiration that no young athlete could help but absorb," Rice
wrote when Rockne died.[17]

Rockne gave only a few hair-raising pep talks to his team,
but the stories of those ascribed to him and his style and ability
as a public speaker led the nation to believe he poured forth emotional harangues at every half time. Rockne would call up the
legend of George Gipp and the imagery of the Four Horsemen
in his business-motivation speeches and have car salesmen on
their feet as he exhorted them to "Win! Win! Win!"[18] When he
died, Rockne was director of sales promotion for the Studebaker
Corporation[19] and made nearly ten times his Notre Dame salary
through that job, his football clinics, writing, and movie consul-
tation.[20]

Rockne's phenomenal success at Notre Dame put him in position for outside income opportunities. In his thirteen seasons
as Notre Dame's head coach, the Irish won 105 games, lost 12,
and tied 5, outscoring their opponents 2,847 to 667 points.[21]

As precise as Rockne was about the nuts and bolts of football, he could be inaccurate, romantic, and theatrical about the
game off the field. Rockne wrote articles for magazines and a column for the Christy Walsh Syndicate as well as a novel, *The Four
Winners*, a thinly disguised and idealized story of Notre Dame
football. His writing helped build his legend by providing readers with the dramatic inside story. In none of these stories does

sentiment overshadow fact as much as in the George Gipp saga. It is, perhaps, the sports story that has had the greatest impact on the public. But it is also a story, including Rice's recollection of it, layered in uncertainty and inconsistency.

Rockne never coached a better player than Gipp. In the football jargon of the time, he was a triple threat, gaining 4,833 all-purpose yards in 26 games with Notre Dame. He also had an enormous talent for cards, pool, and gambling and had little interest in schoolwork or discipline. All of Rockne's accounts of Gipp overlook or minimize these less-illustrious aspects of his life.

Gipp died December 14, 1920, at the age of twenty-five, when a cold and chronic tonsillitis led to pneumonia. He entered the hospital three weeks before his death, just after Notre Dame's game with Northwestern.[22] The Northwestern game had been billed as George Gipp Day by the Notre Dame Alumni Association, but Gipp, who had a cold, did not play until the fourth quarter. With the crowd clamoring for Rockne to put him in the game, the coach relented. Gipp promptly threw touchdown passes of thirty-five and fifty-five yards, the latter the longest in college history to that time.[23] In 1947, Rice reported a remark by Jess Harper, who had preceded Rockne as Notre Dame's coach. Harper contended that football had killed Gipp because "he insisted on playing with impending pneumonia and a temperature above 102."

Gipp might have been remembered only vaguely today as a great football player from the days of leather helmets and dropkicks were it not for the Notre Dame–Army game of 1928. In that game he passed into American folklore. Rockne had his worst team in 1928. The club had lost four games and suffered Notre Dame's first home loss since 1905. Rockne gave the team the nickname Minute Men: he said after it played a minute, the other team scored. In 1928, the Irish faced an undefeated Army team. Rockne evoked the memory of Gipp to spark his players. That much is known to be true. It also is known that Notre Dame's Jack Chevigny yelled something along the lines of "that's one for the Gipper!" when he scored the Irish's first touchdown, and that Johnny O'Brien gained the nickname One-Play when he came off the bench to catch the touchdown pass that gave Notre Dame a 12-6 victory. After that, the various stories and recollections of the Gipper game differ.

Gipp supposedly made a deathbed request of Rockne to ask the Notre Dame players to win a game for him when they were in a tough spot. Whether he actually did, only Rockne could know.[24] Rockne had stooped to bogus stunts before to charge his team emotionally. Before a 1922 game with Georgia Tech, Rockne read to the team a telegram from his ailing son Billy, who was not sick at all. Before unbeaten Notre Dame played Southern California in 1929, Rockne told the players he was quitting because of alumni pressure; he had quit at least four times previously during half-time speeches.[25]

Rice has been credited with making the Gipp story famous, and his version of the tale contains the elements most firmly established in the public mind. Gipp, practically dying in Rockne's arms, whispered, "Some day, Rock, some time—when the going isn't so easy, when the odds are against us, ask a Notre Dame team to win a game for me—for the Gipper. I don't know where I'll be then, Rock, but I'll know about it and I'll be happy." Rockne recalled Gipp's death scene eight years later at the half time of the Army game. The sobbing Irish raced out for the third quarter, and with the knowledge that they played with a twelfth man on their side, upset the Cadets.[26]

The story, with its triumph of spirit over flesh, captured the period's romanticism of college football. The tale seems tailored for (or even by) Rice. But Rice did not break the news of the emotional factor in Notre Dame's upset of Army. Francis Wallace of the *New York Daily News* revealed the story two days after the game.[27] Rice had not attended the game. In his autobiography, published in 1954, Rice related that Rockne stopped by his New York apartment after putting the team to bed the night before the game against Army. There he told Rice of Gipp's request and how he might have to use it the next day.[28] The next day, Rice was in Atlanta covering the Georgia Tech–Vanderbilt game.[29] It seems impossible for Rice to have entertained Rockne late Friday night in New York and then been in Atlanta Saturday afternoon, given that he would have traveled by train.

The Gipp story may be the most famous in the country's sports history, but the most famous lead paragraph on any sports story came from Rice's report on a 1924 Notre Dame–Army game. This time Rice had a direct hand in creating a Notre Dame legend and in placing Rockne and his team in the national spotlight. His story in the *New York Herald-Tribune* began:

> Outlined against a blue-gray October sky, the Four Horsemen rode again. In dramatic lore they are known as Famine, Pestilence, Destruction and Death. These are only aliases. Their real names are Stuhldreher, Miller, Crowley and Layden. They formed the crest of the South Bend cyclone before which another fighting Army football team was swept over the precipice at the Polo Grounds yesterday afternoon as 55,000 spectators peered down on the bewildering panorama spread on the green plain below.

In the next paragraph, 138 words into the story, Rice gave the game's score, a 13-7 Notre Dame victory[30]—a trifle close for a team featuring the Four Horsemen of the Apocalypse in the backfield. The lead might give the copy editor of the 1990s a fit, but at the time it caused a sensation. The story may be the best single example of the impact of newsprint on sports.[31] Red Smith wrote of the Four Horsemen lead, "The magic of the catchwords transformed a gifted, excited, wonderfully coordinated pony backfield into a quartet of immortals."[32] The story pushed Rockne and Notre Dame to a new level of prominence almost overnight, and a publicity photo of the four backs in football gear mounted on horses ensured the immortality Rice's nickname had bestowed on the backfield. In 1925, when the *New York Herald-Tribune* broke the story of Rockne's signing with Columbia, the headline identified the coach as the "Mentor of Notre Dame's Four Horsemen,"[33] even though the four players had graduated the previous spring. In 1926, the American Football League franchise in Brooklyn was called the Horsemen because Harry Stuhldreher and Elmer Layden played with the team.[34]

Rice did not create bricks without straw. The Four Horsemen formed an outstanding backfield and led Notre Dame to an undefeated record and a Rose Bowl victory over Stanford in the 1924 season.[35] Rice's appellation, however, ensured the group could not be forgotten as easily as other aggregations of collegiate backs. Rice quoted Don Miller as saying to him, "Rock put us together in the same backfield but the day you wrote us up as the Four Horsemen, you conferred an immortality on us that gold could never buy. Let's face it. We were good, sure. But we'd have been just as dead two years after graduation as any other backfield if you hadn't painted that tag line on us."[36]

In a 1930 article for *Collier's* on the Four Horsemen, Rockne wrote of Rice's story, "Grantland Rice rose to lyric heights in celebrating their speed, rhythm and precision, winding up a litany of hallelujahs by proclaiming them The Four Horsemen." The phrase, of course, appears in the first sentence of Rice's story, not at the end of a litany of hallelujahs, but such was the drama of Rockne's recollections. Rockne described the Four Horsemen as "young men eminently qualified by temperament, physique and instinctive pacing to complement one another perfectly and thus produce the best coordinated and most picturesque backfield in the recent history of football."[37] Yet he said the backfield on his undefeated 1929 team was better than the Horsemen.[38]

The smoothness with which the Horsemen worked together was their most admired trait. This coordination and emphasis on teamwork at Notre Dame, in effect, made the coach the star, the director behind the gridiron choreography of eleven players. Rice constantly referred to Rockne's teams as smart and wrote of them as though they bore a tag that identified them as the Rockne brand. After watching Notre Dame beat Navy in 1927, Rice wrote, "It was a wonderful sight to see one of Rockne's veteran teams in action. Every cog is in its place and the entire ensemble drives along with the smoothness of the western wind."[39]

"The only qualifications for a lineman are to be big and dumb. To be a back, you only have to be dumb," Rockne said,[40] but his football philosophy seemed adapted from the plots of fairy tales. Rockne thought that cleverness, deception, and speed were better than brawn and bulk.[41] Rice told the story of how he had taken Rockne to a party at which magician Nate Leipsic was entertaining and there pointed out to Rockne that the magician's hand-is-quicker-than-the-eye tricks were comparable to a quarterback's ballhandling. Rice reported that Rockne said his quarterbacks would study with magicians to improve their faking.[42]

Although based on deception, Rockne's football had more spectator appeal than the mash-and-crash running attacks popular before his innovations. The fans could see the ball better, and longer gains happened more frequently. Rockne built his system around the perfect play. If his famous and controversial shift caught the defense out of position, the blockers executed their assignments, and the back read the hole correctly, the runner had no choice but to sprint for a touchdown. Fans enjoyed the dramatic and unpredictable elements of the attack.[43] College teams were discussed in terms of whether they used the Rockne system,[44] and with this appealing brand of football, Rockne exhibited Notre Dame in all regions of the country, until it became something like America's Team.

It came as a shock to the entire country when Rockne died in a plane crash in Kansas on March 31, 1931. Rockne was traveling to Hollywood to work out the details to serve as technical director on a football movie, one for which Rockne wanted Rice to write the script.[45] In his column the day after Rockne's death,

Rice called him "one of the most attractive personalities this generation has developed along any line."[46]

Ten thousand people waited at Dearborn Station in Chicago for the train carrying Rockne's body. Radio carried his funeral services nationwide.[47] In Norway, where Rockne had been born forty-three years earlier, King Haakon posthumously knighted him.[48] The Studebaker Corporation produced a car called the Rockne in 1932. The Liberty ship *Knute Rockne* served in World War II.[49] And for fifty years, the idealistic, romantic image of Rockne has been preserved on film in Pat O'Brien's portrayal of *Knute Rockne—All-American*.[50]

As the football season following Rockne's death approached, Rice wrote of the Notre Dame team, "You can make your guess that this 1931 bunch will give everything they have, feeling in some mysterious way that the spirit of the lost master is still with them in every game and that his keen eyes are still watching every move."[51] In the football of Rice and Rockne, the spirit always triumphed over the flesh.

CHAPTER 9

Rice's Legacy

Grantland Rice made legends of Jack Dempsey, Babe Ruth, Red Grange, Knute Rockne, Bobby Jones, and Bill Tilden. Their formidable athletic talent would not have done the job alone. In the process of his hero building, Rice became something of a legend himself to those in his profession.

John Kieran was the first writer of the *New York Times*'s "Sports of the Times" column and a colleague of Rice. After Rice's death, Kieran wrote of him: "Grant was like Babe Ruth physically. He had enormous endurance and resistance. I was often amazed at how he could talk, drink and work at the same time for days at a time. He could turn out columns while going through a concrete mixer."[1]

One time, however, Rice couldn't turn out his story. He'd sat in a rainstorm watching the 1926 Jack Dempsey–Gene Tunney heavyweight championship fight while nursing a sore throat and a hangover. Rice was too ill to file his overnight story on the fight, so his friend Ring Lardner told him to take a slug of bourbon, go to bed, and he would file the story for him. Lardner, who had bet five hundred dollars on Dempsey (giving two-to-one odds) and thought the fight must have been fixed for Tunney to beat the champion so soundly in the ten-round decision, wrote a story that ran under Rice's byline. It was loaded with between-the-line implications, portraying a lifeless champion and a challenger-turned-champ unable to finish him off.[2] Rice indicated in his autobiography that he had planned a different approach: "It's fine to help build a champion. But when his time comes to step down, as it always will, it's unpleasant to tear him down and bury him. I intended to give Tunney a fitting tribute in my overnight story that historical night. And I intended to go as easy as I could on Dempsey."[3]

This statement defines the sports-reporting philosophy of Rice and, by extension, of many of his colleagues in the 1920s. They built champions. The image of unsurpassed greatness attained by the leading athletes of the Golden Age is more attributable to the influence of sportswriters than to the caliber of the sportsmen. Not to say that the top athletes of period were not outstanding. They were. Yet nearly all of the achievements of the heroes of the Golden Age have been surpassed. That this group from the 1920s continues to be identified as the greatest in their respective sports' stands as a tribute to the strength of the images created by the sportswriters.

These images fell on fertile ground, a virtual hothouse of an environment, perfect for the production of heroes and athletic marvels. Technology allowed workers' time for more leisurely pursuits. The economy boomed, and the spirit of the nation bobbed upward with the weight of war removed. It was a time when the U.S. Supreme Court ruled that major-league baseball was not a business,[4] and a time when sportswriters used a lively language full of color and drama. In 1972, Paul Gallico described the writing in the Golden Age this way: "When Helen Wills played Suzanne Lenglen, when they met for the first time, you would have thought the world was coming to an end if our fine American girl got licked by this dreadful frog, the awful Frenchwoman. That's stupid, when you look at it now, but in those days it was all played that way, for high drama. You try that today and you'd be laughed out of the newspaper office."[5]

Sportswriters like Rice created fame. When Rice labeled the Four Horsemen of Notre Dame, they became a part of national lore, and their coach, Knute Rockne, became a folk hero. Yet

Rockne had enjoyed phenomenal success at Notre Dame for six seasons before Rice's paragraph catapulted his team to national fame. The Horsemen themselves were no physical marvels, as one might expect of football stars. At 164 pounds, fullback Elmer Layden was the heaviest of the quartet.[6] But to Rice's readers, the Horsemen were larger-than-life giants. Only a small fraction of Rice's readers ever saw the Horsemen play. Most of the nation saw them through Rice's words.

The sportswriters of the Golden Age worked in a time when they had a virtual monopoly on sports news. Few fans had means to verify the sportswriters' accounts. They could go to the games, and in response to the sportswriters' stories, more and more did go to see the supermen for themselves. Attendance at University of Illinois football games doubled in the senior season of the well-publicized Red Grange. Jack Dempsey's fights drew crowds previously unmatched for an athletic event. Still, the number of people who saw the Galloping Ghost and the Manassa Mauler was small when compared to the number of those who read about these athletes.

As the most famous and widely read sportswriter of the time, Rice had a greater chance to shape the views of the public than any of his colleagues. For fans without the immediacy and access to sports that television offers today, he brought the games home. An avid horse player, Rice said enthusiasm coupled with purpose formed the best daily double he'd ever seen.[7] He had an upbeat, idealistic outlook with a strong romantic inclination at a time when romanticism remained in vogue. A poem written by Rice about his profession illustrates his attitude:

If somebody whispered to me, "You can have your pick,"
If kind fortune came to woo me, when the gold was thick,
I would still, by hill and hollow, round the world away,
Stirring deeds of contest follow, till I'm bent and gray.
Sport is youth—and youth's eternal, where the flame is bright;

And our hearts will still be vernal when our hair is white.

And though wealth may never love us, say that we have seen

That the sky is blue above us, and the turf is always green.[8]

Rice's work exhibited his personality. He wrote well, had broad command of his subject matter, and understood the need to convey color and excitement to readers. Arthur Daley, who won a Pulitzer Prize for his sports writing in the *New York Times*, wrote of Rice, "There was poetry in Granny's soul and poetry in his pen—or his typewriter."[9] Although he wrote about one million words a year, Rice had the poet's ability to capture in a few words a feeling that condensed images into a phrase. The Galloping Ghost, the Four Horsemen, the Sultan of Swat, all conjure images of athletes in their moments of glory.

Rice viewed sports as a testing ground of the soul. He had an abiding interest in character. When his colleagues rushed to the winners' locker room after a game, Rice walked the other way: "I've learned more from a coach talking with him after losing a game than I ever did in discussing the play that won it for him."[10] Rice's readers learned that Jack Dempsey in the ring had nothing but mayhem on his mind, but outside he was a likable, everyday sort of man. Rice's readers learned that Babe Ruth not only could hit a baseball farther and higher than any man who ever lived but also was deeply devoted to children.

Rice gave his readers and succeeding generations more than a game. He gave them a Golden Age of Sports, a glorious period of athletic heroes. Rice was not the only factor that produced the Golden Age. An army of Rices could arise today and not re-create the athletic exuberance of the 1920s. The factors, and perhaps Rice himself, were unique. The electronic media have changed our lives—and the role of the sportswriter. Readers today see an event at the same time the sportswriter sees it, forcing the sportswriter to explain, probe, and get behind the scenes to remain relevant.

Television also has helped created something of a second Golden Age of Sports, a time when the interest in athletics pervades the country. Sports in the 1990s lack the mass hysteria that accompanied the big sporting events of the 1920s, because commercial athletics have become almost commonplace—and the commercial aspect is apt, because some of our biggest sports heroes seem more like copyrighted trademarks than good ballplayers.

Paul Gallico said he quit as a sportswriter because of the desert month of February. The modern sports calendar has no February. Today, the interest of the sports fan flows through a script of events that defines the seasons as much as the weather—from baseball's opening day, the Masters, Kentucky Derby, Boston Marathon, and NCAA basketball tournament in spring, to the French Open, Belmont Stakes, Wimbledon, Indianapolis 500, baseball's all-star game, and British Open in summer, to the U.S. Open in tennis, and pennant push, playoffs, and World Series in baseball in autumn, to the traditional rivalries and bowl games of college football, NFL playoffs, Super Bowl, Daytona 500, and college-basketball tournaments in winter, with innumerable games on days in between.

Rice, who defined his job as one thrill after another, certainly would find this never-ending story of sports to his liking. If Rice rose anew today, he probably could not, nor would he want to, write exactly as he did in the 1920s. But other aspects of his style, manner, and personality would assure his acclaim as a sports columnist just as they did in the Golden Age. His enthusiasm would protect him from the grind sometimes imposed on sportswriters by the unending cycle of modern sports. No stodgy old-timer trapped in time, Rice looked ahead with an anticipation equal to his reverence for the greats of the past. A few months before his death, Rice wrote in his autobiography: "The best doesn't belong to the past. It is with us now. And even better athletes will be with us on ahead. When we arrive at the top athlete, the Jim Thorpe of the Year 2000, we should really have something."[11]

Rice's attitude would be welcome in a time in which so many sportswriters have forgotten that at the heart of their work lies children's games, full of joy and fun and the excitement and unpredictability of youth. These elements of fun and drama are why sports have fans, why sports pages have readers. Rice became a conduit through which fans, by sharing in his exuberance and knowledge, could enjoy sports.

Could he return to work today, Rice undoubtedly would find that the aspects of commercial sports he disliked have not gone away since he witnessed the dawn of nationwide athletics. When Rice saw the quick-money scoundrels and the hangers-on in Jack Dempsey's entourage following his defeat of Jess Willard, he wrote, "Hail the conquering hero comes, surrounded by a bunch of bums."[12] Today, his words might be different, but he would say the same thing. Rice would be able to raise, in a style that captured the rhythms and moods of today, the same objections and concerns he had in the 1920s.

As he influenced his colleagues during the Golden Age, Rice's work and career remain examples from which modern sportswriters can learn. The loss of immediacy and monopoly brought by television and radio does not preclude writing well on the sports pages. Apt description and deft original phrasing always will be preferable to the clichés that dominate sports reporting. The soul of a poet can impart more about a game than any ream of statistics ever could.

The modern sportswriter who sees little but laughable purple prose in Rice's work should remember the debt owed to Rice. You can often hear the claim that the best writing in newspapers can be found on the sports pages. Not coincidentally, sportswriters have traditionally had more editorial license and leeway than news reporters. At one time, sportswriters habitually abused this freedom, turning out copy riddled with jargon-filled gobbledygook understandable only to sports insiders. But as news writing became more formulaic sportswriters retained some of their freedom, no small thanks to Rice. He used his Vanderbilt education in the classics, his sense of drama, and his connections to the literary elite of his day to bring a respectability and acclaim to sports reporting that it had never had. The quality and popularity of his work gave sports writing direction and, at the same time, justified its continued editorial license.

Rice stands at the forefront of what has become one of the strongest bonds among the people of the United States in the twentieth century: the body of shared knowledge about the heroes and folklore of sport that lies embedded in the national consciousness in a way that transcends the divisive factors of politics, race, religion, and finances. The Sultan of Swat, the Manassa Mauler, the Grand Slam, win one for the Gipper, the Four Horsemen, the long count, the Galloping Ghost—codes words that even today unlock images and feelings in people from coast to coast. Rice's followers in the years since the Golden Age have added to this national treasury the Gashouse Gang, Wilt the Stilt, the boys of summer, the shot heard 'round the world, the Say-Hey Kid, Arnie's Army, the impossible dream, Charlie Hustle.

Today, we have video images that tell our stories as they happen. We saw Bucky Dent's home run over the Green Monster that beat the Red Sox, we saw the ball go through Bill Buckner's legs in the 1986 World Series, we saw John Riggins run for the winning touchdown on fourth down in the Super Bowl, we saw Michael Jordan's jump shot win the national basketball championship for North Carolina. And we can see them again and again and again. Videotapes capture these moments exactly, frozen in time, the whole truth and nothing but the truth. Yet we are not a nation of lawyers.

Perhaps technology has made imagery and storytelling superfluous. Then again, maybe Rice had the right idea. Millions of us saw the Dodgers' Kirk Gibson hobble to the plate and hit the winning home run in the first game of the 1988 World Series. But do we remember it any better today, savor its drama more deeply, for having seen it? Where are the words that capture the moment for us forever, that make the hair on the back of our neck tingle and our throat clutch on a lump? Does hearing how Kirk Gibson felt about hitting that home run make us feel? Perhaps we have given up our stories too easily. Dazzled by an electronic coat of many colors, sportswriters have yielded their birthright and settled for the preciseness of statistics and the cleanliness of quotes. The elements of the stories Rice used to help create the Golden Age still exist in sports—heroes and goats, winners and losers, the rise and fall of fortune, heart and desire and magnificent skill. The stories need to be told, and for a deeper reason than the games themselves.

Notes

Beginnings

1. Ira Berkow, *Red: A Biography of Red Smith* (New York: Times Books, 1986), 105.
2. Robert Kilborn, Jr., "Sports Journalism in the 1920s: A Study of the Interdependence of the Daily Newspaper and the Sports Hero" (Master's thesis, Michigan State Univ., 1972), 142.
3. Robert Lipsyte, *Sports World: An American Dreamland* (New York: Quadrangle, 1975), 170.
4. Fred Russell, *Bury Me in an Old Press Box* (New York: A. S. Barnes, 1957), 201.

1. Grantland Rice

1. "Grantland Rice Every Week," *Collier's*, 15 Nov. 1924, 74.
2. Red Smith, "My Press-Box Memoirs," *Esquire*, Oct. 1975, 202.
3. Lipsyte, *Sports World: An American Dreamland*, 170–72.
4. Grantland Rice, *The Tumult and the Shouting: My Life in Sport* (New York: A. S. Barnes, 1954), 169.
5. Stanley Woodward, *Sports Page* (New York: Simon and Schuster, 1949), 196.
6. Grantland Rice, "The Sporting Thing," *Collier's*, 29 Aug. 1925, 12.
7. Paul Gallico, *The Golden People* (Garden City, N.Y.: Doubleday, 1965), 295.
8. Harry Heath, Jr., and Lou Gelfand, *How To Cover, Write and Edit Sports* (Ames: Iowa State College Press, 1957), 405.
9. Stanley Frank, ed., *Sports Extra: Classics of Sports Reporting* (New York: A. S. Barnes, 1944), 88.
10. Russell, *Bury Me*, 195.

11. Red Smith, *To Absent Friends from Red Smith* (New York: Atheneum, 1982), 45. (From 20 Aug. 1954 *New York Herald-Tribune* column "A Letter About Granny.")

12. Bob Cooke, ed., *Wake Up the Echoes: From the Sports Pages of the New York Herald-Tribune* (Garden City, N.Y.: Hanover House, 1956), 239. (From Red Smith column "At Granny's School," Nov. 1955).

13. Jerome Holtzman, ed., *No Cheering in the Press Box* (New York: Holt, Rinehart and Winston, 1973), 30.

14. Grantland Rice, "Too Much Money," *Collier's,* 12 Sept. 1925, 12.

15. Grantland Rice, "The Sportlight," *New York Herald-Tribune,* 10 Aug. 1927, 21.

16. Ibid., 6 Oct. 1927, 28.

17. Dave Camerer, ed., *The Best of Grantland Rice* (New York: Franklin Watts, 1963), 138, 212.

18. Paul Gallico, *Farewell To Sport* (New York: Alfred A. Knopf, 1938; reprint, Freeport, N.Y.: Books for Libraries Press, 1970), 70.

19. Rice, *The Tumult and the Shouting,* 37, 54.

20. Ibid., xvi.

21. Grantland Rice, "My Greatest Thrill in 22 Years of Sport," *American Magazine,* May 1924, 41.

22. Grantland Rice, "Can Dempsey Come Back?" *Collier's,* 12 June 1926, 7.

23. Camerer, *The Best of Grantland Rice,* 7–8.

24. John Devaney and Burt Goldblatt, *The World Series: A Complete Pictorial History* (New York: Rand McNally, 1976), 94.

25. Gerald Astor, *The Baseball Hall of Fame Fiftieth Anniversary Book* (New York: Prentice-Hall, 1988), 91.

26. Smith, *To Absent Friends,* 42. (From "Grantland Rice," *New York Herald-Tribune* column, 8 Aug. 1954).

27. John McCallum and Charles H. Pearson, *College Football U.S.A.—Official Book of the National Football Foundation* (New York: Hall of Fame Publishing, 1971), 229.

28. Arthur Daley, "Sports of the Times," *New York Times,* 15 July 1954, 30.

29. Rice, *The Tumult and the Shouting,* 7.

30. Berkow, *Red: A Biography,* 106.

31. Grantland Rice, "You Can't Win Without It," *Collier's,* 6 Dec. 1924, 16.

32. Camerer, *The Best of Grantland Rice,* 190.

33. Lipsyte, *Sports World: An American Dreamland,* 172.

34. Woodward, *Sports Page,* 61.

35. Stanley Walker, *City Editor* (New York: Frederick A. Stokes Co., 1939), 123–24.

36. Holtzman, *No Cheering*, 126.
37. Advertisement, *New York Herald-Tribune*, 23 Sept. 1927, 8.

2. The Golden Age

1.   Frank, *Sports Extra*, 38–39.
2.   Woodward, *Sports Page*, 49–50.
3.   Paul Gallico, "The Golden Decade," *Saturday Evening Post*, 5 Sept. 1931, 12.
4.   Frederick L. Allen, *Only Yesterday: An Informal History of the 1920s* (New York: Harper and Brothers, 1931), 224.
5.   Grantland Rice, "The Return to Sport," *Country Life*, June 1919, 40, 43.
6.   Grantland Rice, "How Uncle Sam Created an Army of Athletes," *Scientific American*, 8 Feb. 1919, 114.
7.   Randy Roberts, *Jack Dempsey: The Manassa Mauler* (Baton Rouge: Louisiana State Univ. Press, 1979), 66.
8.   Max Lerner, *American as a Civilization: Life and Thought in the United States Today* (New York: Simon and Schuster, 1957), 818.
9.   Benjamin G. Rader, *American Sports: From the Age of Folk Games to the Age of Spectators* (Englewood Cliffs, N.J.: Prentice-Hall, 1983), 176–77.
10. Camerer, *The Best of Grantland Rice*, 227–28.
11. Douglas A. Noverr and Lawrence E. Ziewacz, *The Games They Played: Sports in American History, 1865–1980* (Chicago: Nelson-Hall, 1983), 68–70.
12. Allison Danzig and Peter Brandwein, eds., *Sport's Golden Age: A Close-Up of the Fabulous Twenties* (New York: Harper and Row, 1948; reprint, Freeport, N.Y.: Books for Libraries Press, 1969), 1–2.
13. Rice, "My Greatest Thrill," 41.
14. In a famous Ruth anecdote, perhaps apocryphal, a reporter asked Ruth how a baseball player could justify making a larger salary than Herbert Hoover, the president of the United States. Ruth replied earnestly, "Hell, I had a better year than he did."
15. George Gipe, *The Great American Sports Book* (Garden City, N.Y.: Doubleday, 1978), 92.
16. "Sports Dig Ever More Deeply into Newspaper's Editorial Space," *Editor and Publisher*, 28 Apr. 1928, 44.
17. John R. Tunis, "Gas and the Games," *Saturday Evening Post*, 25 Jan. 1930, 44.
18. Heath and Gelfand, *How To Cover*, 6.
19. Tunis, "Gas and the Games," 13.
20. Allen, *Only Yesterday*, 188.
21. Walker, *City Editor*, 116, 120.
22. Lester Jordan, "Sports Reporting Was a Scholarly Occupation Fifty Years Ago," *Editor and Publisher*, 2 July 1927, 9.

23. Lerner, *American as a Civilization*, 804.

24. Holtzman, *No Cheering*, 146.

25. Gallico, *The Golden People*, 293–95.

26. John Underwood, "Was He the Greatest of All Time?" *Sports Illustrated*, 4 Sept. 1985, 115.

27. Gallico, *The Golden People*, 293.

28. In the latter half of the 1920s, Rice's column, "The Sportlight," and McGeehan's column, "Down the Line," often ran daily on the same page in the *New York Herald-Tribune*.

29. Woodward, *Sports Page*, 59–60.

30. Cooke, *Wake Up the Echoes*, 71.

31. Jonathan Yardley, *Ring: A Biography of Ring Lardner* (New York: Random House, 1977), 24.

32. Frank, *Sports Extra*, 38.

33. Heath and Gelfand, *How To Cover*, 5.

34. Rice, *The Tumult and the Shouting*, 137.

35. Danzig and Brandwein, *Sport's Golden Age*, ix.

36. Some feel the quality of Rice's poetry has been ignored because of his profession and his use of verse to comment on athletics. Arthur Daley wrote, "Technically speaking, [Rice] was one of America's great poets, a talent obscured by the richness of his prose and the field in which he operated" ("Granny's Poetic Pen," *New York Times*, 21 Nov. 1954, 18[G]).

37. Camerer, *The Best of Grantland Rice*, 5.

38. Reinhold Niebuhr, "Heroes and Hero Worship," *Nation*, 23 Feb. 1921, 293.

3. Jack Dempsey

1. Rader, *American Sports*, 189. (More than forty years after the fight, Jack Kearns, Dempsey's manager, said he had coated the tape on Dempsey's hands with plaster of paris because he had bet ten thousand dollars at ten-to-one odds that Dempsey would knock out Willard in the first round.)

2. Camerer, *The Best of Grantland Rice*, 33.

3. Randy Roberts, "Jack Dempsey: An American Hero in the 1920s," *Journal of Popular Culture* 8 (Fall 1974): 413–59.

4. Rader, *American Sports*, 187.

5. Camerer, *The Best of Grantland Rice*, 34.

6. Allen, *Only Yesterday*, 210.

7. Fred Russell, *I'll Try Anything Twice* (Nashville, Tenn.: McQuiddy Press, 1945), 78.

8. Gallico, *Farewell to Sport*, 92. (Gene Tunney defeated Tom Heeney in this fight.)

9.   Grantland Rice, "Boxing for a Million Dollars," *American Review of Reviews*, Oct. 1926, 420.

10.   Roberts, *Jack Dempsey: The Manassa Mauler*, 268.

11.   Roberts, "Jack Dempsey," 414–60.

12.   Rice's report on the fight in the *New York Herald-Tribune* as cited in Roberts, *Jack Dempsey: The Manassa Mauler*, 98.

13.   Rader, *American Sports*, 189–90.

14.   Rice, *The Tumult and the Shouting*, 119.

15.   Roberts, "Jack Dempsey," 418–64, 415–61.

16.   Roberts, *Jack Dempsey: The Manassa Mauler*, 180, 188.

17.   Rice, *The Tumult and the Shouting*, 121.

18.   Camerer, *The Best of Grantland Rice*, 33.

19.   Roberts, "Jack Dempsey," 420–66.

20.   Rice, "Boxing for a Million Dollars," 419.

21.   Grantland Rice, "If They Don't Think, They Lose," *Collier's*, 24 Jan. 1925, 17.

22.   Grantland Rice, "Dempsey Couldn't Knock Him Down," *Collier's*, 31 Jan. 1925, 20.

23.   Grantland Rice, "Will Their Crowns Stay On?" *Collier's*, 27 Feb. 1926, 29.

24.   Rice, "Can Dempsey Come Back?" 7.

25.   Rice, "The Sportlight," 2 Sept. 1926, 21.

26.   Rice, "Can Dempsey Come Back?" 7.

27.   Rice, "The Sportlight," 23 Sept. 1926, 24.

28.   Grantland Rice, "150,000 at Fight Tonight; Bettors Turn to Dempsey," *New York Herald-Tribune*, 22 Sept. 1927, 27.

29.   Grantland Rice, "Punch and Fighting Instinct Dempsey's Big Assets Tomorrow," *New York Herald-Tribune*, 21 Sept. 1927, 25.

30.   Grantland Rice, "Jack Dempsey Has Even Chance To Regain Crown, Rice Thinks," *New York Herald-Tribune*, 20 Sept. 1927, 29.

31.   Rader, *American Sports*, 192.

32.   Grantland Rice, "Tunney Wins From Dempsey; Keeps Title; 145,000 in Chicago Pay $3,000,000 To See Battle," *New York Herald-Tribune*, 23 Sept. 1927, 25. (W. O. McGeehan's round-by-round account of the fight, which accompanied Rice's story, did not mention the long count either.)

33.   Grantland Rice, "Tunney's Fighting Finish After Knock-Down in Seventh Proves Right to Title of Champion," *New York Herald-Tribune*, 24 Sept. 1927, 16.

34.   Grantland Rice, "Rocks in the Glory Path," *Collier's*, 5 Mar. 1927, 28.

35.   Roberts, *Jack Dempsey: The Manassa Mauler*, 59, 77.

36.   Camerer, *The Best of Grantland Rice*, 38.

37.   Grantland Rice, "Dempsey Whips Sharkey by Seventh-Round Knock-
      out," *New York Herald-Tribune,* 22 July 1927, 1, 19(A).
38.   Grantland Rice, "Shift in Betting and Questionable Defeat of Sharkey
      Raise Rumors Dempsey Had To Win," *New York Herald-Tribune,* 23 July
      1927, 12(A).
39.   Rice, "The Sportlight," 29 July 1927, 18(A).
40.   Rice, "Shift in Betting," 12(A).
41.   Rice, "The Sportlight," 29 Sept. 1927, 28.
42.   Grantland Rice, "Was Jack the Giant Killer?" *Collier's,* 28 May 1927, 9.
43.   Rice, "The Sportlight," 8 Aug. 1928, 19.
44.   Rice, *The Tumult and the Shouting,* 116.

4. Babe Ruth

1.   Rice, *The Tumult and the Shouting,* 101–2.
2.   Ibid., 104–5.
3.   Robert W. Creamer, "And Along Came Ruth," *Sports Illustrated,* 18 Mar.
      1974, 86.
4.   Richard M. Cohen, Jordan A. Deutsch and David S. Neft, *The Sports
      Encyclopedia: Baseball* (New York: Gossett and Dunlap, 1982), 188–91.
5.   Robert W. Creamer, "Hit Opening in New York," *Sports Illustrated,* 25
      Mar. 1974, 41.
6.   Astor, *Baseball Hall of Fame,* 120.
7.   Gallico, "The Golden Decade," 12.
8.   Cohen, *Jordan A. Deutsch and David S. Neft,* 124.
9.   Creamer, "Hit Opening in New York," 42. (The Yankees drew 1,289,422
      spectators in 1920 to break the attendance record of 910,000 set by the
      1908 New York Giants, the only major league team before 1920 to attract
      more than 700,000 fans in a season.)
10.   Creamer, "And Along Came Ruth," 90.
11.   Marshall Smelser, *The Life that Ruth Built* (New York: Quadrangle, 1975),
      115.
12.   Cohen, *Jordan A. Deutsch and David S. Neft,* 132.
13.   Noverr and Ziewacz, *The Games They Played,* 73.
14.   Camerer, *The Best of Grantland Rice,* 239. (Rice died the year Hank Aaron,
      who surpassed Ruth's career home run record, broke into the major
      leagues.)
15.   Grantland Rice, "Ruth Hits Three Home Runs As Yankees Win, 10-5,"
      New York Herald-Tribune, 7 Oct. 1926, 1, 15.
16.   Rice, "The Sportlight," 13 Oct. 1926, 30.

17. Grantland Rice, "St. Louis Cardinals Win Series, Beat Yankees, 3-2," *New York Herald-Tribune*, 11 Oct. 1926, 21.
18. Grantland Rice, "Yankees Win Third in Row as Pennock Stills Pirates, 8 to 1," *New York Herald-Tribune*, 8 Oct. 1927, 1.
19. Grantland Rice, "Yankees Win from Pirates Again, 6-2, as Pipgras Stars," *New York Herald-Tribune*, 7 Oct. 1927, 1, 25.
20. Cohen, Jordan A. Deutsch and David S. Neft, 152.
21. Astor, *Baseball Hall of Fame*, 124.
22. Creamer, "Hit Opening in New York," 58.
23. Smelser, *The Life that Ruth Built*, 566–67.
24. Rice, "The Sportlight," 19 Oct. 1926, 28.
25. Tom Meany, *Babe Ruth* (New York: A. S. Barnes, 1947), 99.
26. Cohen, Jordan A. Deutsch and David S. Neft, 144.
27. Rice, "The Sportlight," 14 Aug. 1925, 12.
28. Meany, *Babe Ruth*, 125.
29. Rice, *The Tumult and the Shouting*, 295.
30. Rice, "The Sportlight," 29 Oct. 1925, 18.
31. Grantland Rice, "What Draws the Crowds?" *Collier's*, 20 June 1925, 10.
32. Edward Ehre and Irving T. Marsh, eds., *Best Sports Stories—1949 Edition* (New York: E. P. Dutton, 1949), 40–41.
33. Wells Twombly, *Two Hundred Years of Sport in America: A Pageant of a Nation at Play* (New York: McGraw-Hill, 1976), 130–31.
34. Rice, "What Draws the Crowds?" 44.
35. "Ruth Keeps Air Mail Promise of Homer for Boy Near Death," *New York Herald-Tribune*, 7 Oct. 1926, 1.
36. Rice, *The Tumult and the Shouting*, 111.
37. Rice, "What Draws the Crowds?" 10.
38. Grantland Rice, "There's No Such Word As Quit," *Collier's*, 28 Feb. 1925, 13.
39. Rice, "The Sportlight," 13 Oct. 1926, 30.
40. Ibid., 27 Sept. 1927, 30.
41. Ehre and Marsh, *Best Sports Stories*, 39–40, 42.

5. Bobby Jones

1. Camerer, *The Best of Grantland Rice*, 70.
2. Cooke, *Wake Up the Echoes*, 134.
3. Herbert Warren Wind, *The Story of American Golf* (New York: Alfred A. Knopf, 1975), 33.
4. Robert Scharff, ed., *Golf Magazine's Encyclopedia of Golf* (New York: Harper and Row, 1970), 15, 142, 162.

5.   Grantland Rice, "To Beard the Lion," *Collier's*, 15 May 1926, 26.
6.   Grantland Rice, "Bobby Jones Wins National Amateur Golf Champion-ship, 8 & 7," *New York Herald-Tribune*, 28 Aug. 1927, 1(B).
7.   Wind, *The Story of American Golf*, 162, 198–99.
8.   Cooke, *Wake Up the Echoes*, 133.
9.   Grantland Rice, "Bobby Jones Turns Back Evans' Brilliant Bid, Eliminating Chick, 3 & 2, in Title Golf," *New York Herald-Tribune*, 17 Sept. 1926, 23.
10. Grantland Rice, "Jones and Von Elm Reach Final for National Amateur Golf Crown by Decisive Victories," *New York Herald-Tribune*, 18 Sept. 1926, 14.
11. Grantland Rice, "Von Elm Wins Bobby Jones's Amateur Title," *New York Herald-Tribune*, 19 Sept. 1926, 1, 16.
12. Rice, "Bobby Jones Wins National Amateur," 1, 4(B).
13. Camerer, *The Best of Grantland Rice*, 67–68.
14. Grantland Rice, "Born to the Purple," *Collier's*, 12 Mar. 1927, 16.
15. Grantland Rice, "Playing Short Pitches Correctly Made Bobby Jones Invincible," *New York Herald-Tribune*, 29 Aug. 1927, 12.
16. Lipsyte, *Sports World: An American Dreamland*, 172–73.
17. Grantland Rice, "Ace of Clubs," *Collier's*, 27 Sept. 1930, 15.
18. Rice, "The Sportlight," 26 July 1927, 19.
19. Camerer, *The Best of Grantland Rice*, 175.
20. Scharff, *Golf Magazine's Encyclopedia of Golf*, 16. (Today, the United States has more than 12,400 golf courses.)
21. Cooke, *Wake Up the Echoes*, 120, 146.
22. Twombly, *Two Hundred Years of Sport*, 169–71.
23. Rice, *The Tumult and the Shouting*, 74.
24. Gallico, *Farewell to Sport*, 71.
25. John R. Tunis, *Sports: Heroics and Hysterics* (New York: John Day, 1928), 27.
26. Wind, *The Story of American Golf*, 162.
27. Grantland Rice, "The Old Familiar Faces," *Collier's*, 2 Jan. 1926, 21.
28. Rice, "Ace of Clubs," 15.
29. Camerer, *The Best of Grantland Rice*, 173.
30. Ibid., 181.
31. Scharff, *Golf Magazine's Encyclopedia of Golf*, 145.
32. Rice, *The Tumult and the Shouting*, 155.
33. Camerer, *The Best of Grantland Rice*, 175.

6. Bill Tilden

1.   Rice, "The Sportlight," 29 Sept. 1926, 23.
2.   Twombly, *Two Hundred Years of Sport*, 163.

3.   Grantland Rice, "Big Bill Tilden," *Collier's*, 29 Nov. 1924, 45.

4.   Gallico, *The Golden People*, 45.

5.   Rader, *American Sports*, 220.

6.   Frank Deford, "Hero with a Tragic Flaw," *Sports Illustrated*, 13 Jan. 1975, 52.

7.   Rice, "Big Bill Tilden," 17.

8.   Allison Danzig and Peter Brandwein, eds., *Sport's Golden Age: A Close-Up of the Fabulous '20s* (New York: Harper and Row, 1948; reprint, Freeport, N.Y.: Books for Libraries Press, 1969), 218.

9.   Gallico, *The Golden People*, 121.

10.   Tunis, *Sports: Heroics and Hysterics*, 25.

11.   Cooke, *Wake Up the Echoes*, 129.

12.   Grantland Rice, "The Thrill of a Hard Fight," *Collier's*, 14 Nov. 1925, 14.

13.   Rice, "Big Bill Tilden," 45.

14.   Grantland Rice, "How To Be a Champion," *Collier's*, 2 May 1925, 10.

15.   Rice, "The Sportlight," 12 Aug. 1927, 17.

16.   Grantland Rice, "If They Don't Think," 17.

17.   Rice, "Big Bill Tilden," 45.

18.   Deford, "Hero with a Tragic Flaw," 54.

19.   Fred Hawthorne, "Tilden Beaten; Three Frenchmen in Semi-Final," *New York Herald-Tribune*, 17 Sept. 1926, 1.

20.   Rice, "The Sportlight," 25 Sept. 1926, 14.

21.   Deford, "Hero with a Tragic Flaw," 54.

22.   Grantland Rice, "The French Wave," *Collier's*, 14 May 1927, 10.

23.   Rice, "The Sportlight," 12 Aug. 1927, 17.

24.   Rice, "The French Wave," 10.

25.   Deford, "Hero with a Tragic Flaw," 57.

26.   Rader, *American Sports*, 222–23.

27.   Deford, "Hero with a Tragic Flaw," 57.

28.   Rice, "The Sportlight," 21 Aug. 1928, 22.

29.   Rice, *The Tumult and the Shouting*, 165.

30.   Frank Deford, *Big Bill Tilden: The Triumphs and the Tragedy* (New York: Simon and Schuster, 1975), 247–49, 259.

31.   Rice, *The Tumult and the Shouting*, 158–59, 168.

32.   Rice, "Will Their Crowns Stay On?" 29.

33.   Deford, *Big Bill Tilden*, 156.

7. Red Grange

1.   Ivan N. Kaye, *Good Clean Violence: A History of College Football* (Philadelphia: J. B. Lippincott, 1973), 81.

2.   Underwood, "Was He the Greatest," 115. (Although Warren Brown of the *Chicago Tribune* and Charlie Dunkley of the Associated Press some-times have been credited with creating Grange's most enduring nick-name, it is generally accepted that Rice was the first to call Grange the Galloping Ghost.)

3.   Grantland Rice, "Is Grange the Greatest?" *Collier's*, 20 Dec. 1924, 14, 38.

4.   Grantland Rice, "Grange Flashes Brilliantly in Final Contest," *New York Herald-Tribune*, 22 Nov. 1925, 3(J).

5.   Underwood, "Was He the Greatest," 118.

6.   Rice, "Is Grange the Greatest?" 14.

7.   Kaye, *Good Clean Violence*, 98.

8.   Underwood, "Was He the Greatest," 116.

9.   Rice, "The Sportlight," 27 Nov. 1925, 20.

10. Underwood, "Was He the Greatest," 116.

11. Grantland Rice, "Yale Proves It Has One of the Country's Great Teams in Day of Startling Football Results," *New York Herald-Tribune*, 2 Nov. 1925, 18.

12. Underwood, "Was He the Greatest," 117.

13. John D. McCallum, *Big Ten Football* (Radnor, Pa.: Chilton Book, 1976), 32.

14. Camerer, *The Best of Grantland Rice*, 134.

15. Rice, "Is Grange the Greatest?" 38.

16. Grantland Rice, "The Stuff Men Are Made Of," *Collier's*, 24 Oct. 1925, 27.

17. Grantland Rice, "Their Greatest Moments," *Collier's*, 16 May 1925, 20. (Written about Grange's game-winning touchdown run late in the fourth quarter of the 1924 Illinois-Chicago game.)

18. Grantland Rice, "Weaving Grange-Like 82-Yard Run by Slagle Is High-light of Tigers' Decisive Triumph," *New York Herald-Tribune*, 15 Nov. 1925, 3(J).

19. Grantland Rice, "Collier's All-America Football Team," *Collier's*, 19 Dec. 1925, 7.

20. "738,555 Gridiron Fans Have Paid To See Grange," *New York Herald-Tribune*, 25 Nov. 1925, 20.

21. "Want Grange in Congress," *New York Times*, 11 Nov. 1925, 20.

22. "70,000 See Grange Win, 19-7," *New York Herald-Tribune*, 7 Dec. 1925, 1.

23. Gipe, *The Great American Sports Book*, 92.

24. Rice, "Is Grange the Greatest?" 14.

25. Camerer, *The Best of Grantland Rice*, 128, 132–33.

26. Rice, "Grange Flashes Brilliantly," 3(J).

27. George Sullivan, *The Great Running Backs* (New York: G. Putnam's Sons, 1972), 26, 30.

28. Rader, *American Sports*, 185.
29. Grantland Rice, "The Pigskin Ballyho," *Collier's*, 18 Sept. 1926, 20.
30. Rader, *American Sports*, 185.
31. Rice, "The Sportlight," 29 Dec. 1925, 18.
32. Ibid., 27 Nov. 1925, 20.
33. Grantland Rice, "More Athletic Activity and Interest Were Crowded into 1925 Than in any Previous Year," *New York Herald-Tribune*, 27 Dec. 1925, 4(J). (In a tour that has been called "the seventeen days that made pro football," the Bears played ten games. Grange received 50 percent of the gate receipts from the tour, with his business manager, C. C. Pyle, getting 40 percent of Grange's take.)
34. Underwood, "Was He the Greatest," 118.
35. Rice, "The Sportlight," 18 Dec. 1925, 25.
36. Sullivan, *The Great Running Backs*, 30.
37. Grantland Rice, "Have You Ever Seen Their Equals?" *Collier's*, 22 Nov. 1924, 12.
38. Rice, "Is Grange the Greatest?" 14.
39. Rice, "The Sportlight," 6 Nov. 1925, 22.
40. Camerer, *The Best of Grantland Rice*, 132, 135.
41. Rice, "The Sportlight," 27 Nov. 1925, 20.
42. Ibid., 5 Dec. 1925, 17.
43. Ibid., 25 Dec. 1925, 20.
44. Rice, *The Tumult and the Shouting*, 210–11.
45. McCallum and Pearson, *College Football U.S.A.*, 550.
46. Underwood, "Was He the Greatest," 120.
47. Rice, "The Sportlight," 17 Dec. 1925, 25.

8. Knute Rockne

1. Twombly, *Two Hundred Years of Sport*, 145.
2. McCallum and Pearson, *College Football U.S.A.*, 161, 236.
3. Twombly, *Two Hundred Years of Sport*, 209.
4. Michael R. Steele, *Knute Rockne: A Bio-Bibliography* (Westport, Conn.: Greenwood Press, 1983), 24, 33, 39.
5. Berkow, *Red: A Biography*, 22.
6. Rice, "The Sportlight," 15 Dec. 1925, 25.
7. Grantland Rice, "Under New Management," *Collier's*, 10 Oct. 1931, 23.
8. Knute Rockne, *Coaching: The Way of the Winner* (New York: Devin Adair, 1929), 159–60.
9. John R. Tunis, "The Newspapers and Sport," *Outlook and Independent*, 8 Jan. 1930, 68.

10.   Alfred S. Dashiell, "Football—Overgrown Darling of the Press," *Independent,* 6 Nov. 1926, 520.

11.   Steele, *Knute Rockne,* 48.

12.   Rice, *The Tumult and the Shouting,* 222–23.

13.   Danzig and Brandwein, *Sport's Golden Age,* 3.

14.   Grantland Rice, "Notre Dame Crushes Navy 19-6 With Rally in the Second Half," *New York Herald-Tribune,* 16 Oct. 1927, 2(B).

15.   Rice, "Under New Management," 23.

16.   Rice, "The Sportlight," 12 Dec. 1925, 16. (In December of 1925, Rockne signed a twenty-five-thousand-dollar contract that more than doubled his Notre Dame salary, but with the stipulation that the pact with Columbia would not be binding unless Notre Dame released him from his current contract. News leaked before Rockne could get that permission, though, and after patching things up with Notre Dame, he backed out the Columbia deal. He did the same thing with Ohio State in 1928.)

17.   Camerer, *The Best of Grantland Rice,* 188.

18.   Steele, *Knute Rockne,* 15, 42.

19.   Coles Phinizy, "We Know of Knute, Yet Know Him Not," *Sports Illustrated,* 10 Sept. 1979, 112.

20.   Frank, *Sports Extra,* 156.

21.   McCallum and Pearson, *College Football U.S.A.,* 168, 173.

22.   Steele, *Knute Rockne,* 18–19, 23.

23.   Coles Phinizy, "Win One for the Gipper," *Sports Illustrated,* 17 Sept. 1979, 47.

24.   Steele, *Knute Rockne,* 39, 182.

25.   Phinizy, "We Know of Knute," 108–9.

26.   Rice, *The Tumult and the Shouting,* 183–84.

27.   Steele, *Knute Rockne,* 41.

28.   Rice, *The Tumult and the Shouting,* 182–83.

29.   Grantland Rice, "Engineers Ramble Over Vandy," *New York Herald-Tribune,* 11 Nov. 1928, 1(D).

30.   Rice, *The Tumult and the Shouting,* 177.

31.   Noverr and Ziewacz, *The Games They Played,* 82.

32.   Berkow, *Red: A Biography,* 22.

33.   "Mentor of Notre Dame's Four Horsemen To Coach at Columbia," *New York-Herald Tribune,* 12 Dec. 1925, 1.

34.   Gipe, *The Great American Sports Book,* 138.

35.   Allison Danzig, *Oh, How They Played the Game: The Early Days of Football and the Heroes Who Made It Great* (New York: Macmillan, 1971), 255.

36.   Rice, *The Tumult and the Shouting,* 181.

37. Kenneth McArdle, ed., *A Cavalcade of Collier's* (New York: A. S. Barnes, 1959), 287–88.

38. McCallum and Pearson, *College Football U.S.A.,* 207.

39. Rice, "Notre Dame Crushes Navy," 1(B).

40. Gipe, *The Great American Sports Book,* 92.

41. Steele, *Knute Rockne,* 31.

42. Rice, *The Tumult and the Shouting,* 185.

43. Steele, *Knute Rockne,* 16–17, 25.

44. Gallico, "The Golden Decade," 124.

45. Rice, *The Tumult and the Shouting,* 191–92.

46. Camerer, *The Best of Grantland Rice,* 187.

47. Twombly, *Two Hundred Years of Sport,* 148.

48. Steele, *Knute Rockne,* 3.

49. Phinizy, "We Know of Knute," 102.

50. Steele, *Knute Rockne,* 36.

51. Rice, "Under New Management," 23.

9. Rice's Legacy

1. Camerer, *The Best of Grantland Rice,* 1.

2. Yardley, *Ring,* 309.

3. Rice, *The Tumult and the Shouting,* 150.

4. Richard Lipsky, *How We Play the Game: Why Sports Dominate American Life* (Boston: Beacon Press, 1981), 5. (This ruling is one in the long judicial history of the players' movement. At that time, a professional player was tied to his team for life unless he was traded, sold, or released. The U.S. Supreme Court ruled in this case that baseball was not a business engaged in interstate commerce and therefore was not subject to antitrust sanctions.)

5. Holtzman, *No Cheering,* 72.

6. Steele, *Knute Rockne,* 31.

7. Camerer, *The Best of Grantland Rice,* 7.

8. Russell, *Bury Me,* 227.

9. Daley, "Granny's Poetic Pen," 18(G).

10. Rice, *The Tumult and the Shouting,* 192.

11. Ibid., 355.

12. Roberts, *Jack Dempsey: The Manassa Mauler,* 65.

Bibliography

Books

Allen, Frederick B. *Only Yesterday: An Informal History of the 1920s.* New York: Harper and Brothers, 1931.

Astor, Gerald. *The Baseball Hall of Fame Fiftieth Anniversary Book.* New York: Prentice-Hall, 1988.

Berkow, Ira. *Red: A Biography of Red Smith.* New York: Times Books, 1986.

Camerer, Dave, ed. *The Best of Grantland Rice.* New York: Franklin Watts, 1963.

Cooke, Bob, ed. *Wake Up the Echoes: From the Sports Pages of the New York Herald-Tribune.* Garden City, N.Y.: Hanover House, 1956.

Danzig, Allison. *Oh, How They Played the Game: The Early Days of Football and the Heroes Who Made it Great.* New York: Macmillan, 1971.

Danzig, Allison, and Peter Brandwein, eds. *Sport's Golden Age: A Close-Up of the Fabulous Twenties.* New York: Harper and Row, 1948. Reprint. Freeport, N.Y.: Books for Libraries Press, 1969.

Deford, Frank. *Big Bill Tilden: The Triumphs and the Tragedy.* New York: Simon and Schuster, 1975.

Deutsch, Jordan A., David S. Neft, and Richard M. Cohen. *The Sports Encyclopedia: Baseball.* New York: Grossett and Dunlap, 1982.

Devaney, John, and Burt Goldblatt. *The World Series: A Complete Pictorial History.* New York: Randy McNally, 1976.

Frank, Stanley, ed. *Sports Extra: Classics of Sports Reporting.* New York: A. S. Barnes, 1944.

Gallico, Paul. *Farewell to Sport.* New York: Alfred A. Knopf, 1938. Reprint. Freeport, N.Y.: Books for Libraries Press, 1970.

———. *The Golden People.* Garden City, N.Y.: Doubleday, 1965.

Gipe, George. *The Great American Sports Book.* Garden City, N.Y.: Doubleday, 1978.

Heath, Harry E., Jr., and Lou Gelfand. *How To Cover, Write and Edit Sports.* Ames: Iowa State College Press, 1957.

Holtzman, Jerome, ed. *No Cheering in the Press Box.* New York: Holt, Rinehart and Winston, 1973.

Kaye, Ivan N. *Good Clean Violence: A History of College Football.* Philadelphia: J. B. Lippincott, 1973.

Lerner, Max. *America as a Civilization: Life and Thought in the United States Today.* New York: Simon and Schuster, 1957.

Lipsky, Richard. *How We Play the Game: Why Sports Dominate American Life.* Boston: Beacon Press, 1981.

Lipsyte, Robert. *Sports World: An American Dreamland.* New York: Quadrangle, 1975.

Marsh, Irving T., and Edward Ehre, eds. *Best Sports Stories—1949 Edition.* New York: E. P. Dutton, 1949.

McArdle, Kenneth, ed. *A Cavalcade of Collier's.* New York: A. S. Barnes, 1959.

McCallum, Jack. *Big Ten Football.* Radnor, Pa.: Chilton Book, 1976.

McCallum, Jack, and Charles H. Pearson. *College Football U.S.A.—Official Book of the National Football Foundation.* New York: Hall of Fame Publishing, 1971.

Meany, Tom. *Babe Ruth.* New York: A. S. Barnes, 1947.

Noverr, Douglas A., and Lawrence E. Ziewacz. *The Games They Played: Sports in American History, 1865-1980.* Chicago: Nelson-Hall, 1983.

Rader, Benjamin G. *American Sports: From the Age of Folk Games to the Age of Spectators.* Englewood Cliffs, N.J.: Prentice-Hall, 1983.

Rice, Grantland. *The Tumult and the Shouting: My Life in Sport.* New York: A. S. Barnes, 1954.

Roberts, Randy. *Jack Dempsey: The Manassa Mauler.* Baton Rouge: Louisiana State Univ. Press, 1979.

Rockne, Knute. *Coaching: The Way of the Winner.* New York: Devin Adair, 1929.

Russell, Fred. *Bury Me in an Old Press Box.* New York: A. S. Barnes, 1957.

———. *I'll Try Anything Twice.* Nashville, Tenn.: McQuiddy Press, 1945.

Scharff, Robert, ed. *Golf Magazine's Encyclopedia of Golf.* New York: Harper and Row, 1970.

Smelser, Marshall. *The Life That Ruth Built.* New York: Quadrangle, 1975.

Smith, Red. *To Absent Friends from Red Smith.* New York: Atheneum, 1982.

Steele, Michael R. *Knute Rockne: A Bio-Bibliography.* Westport, Conn.: Greenwood Press, 1983.

Sullivan, George. *The Great Running Backs.* New York: G. P. Putnam's Sons, 1972.

Tunis, John R. *Sports: Heroics and Hysterics.* New York: John Day, 1928.

Twombly, Wells. *Two Hundred Years of Sport in America: A Pageant of a Nation at Play.* New York: McGraw-Hill, 1976.

Walker, Stanley. *City Editor.* New York: Frederick A. Stokes, 1939.

Wind, Herbert Warren. *The Story of American Golf.* New York: Alfred A. Knopf, 1975.

Woodward, Stanley. *Sports Page.* New York: Simon and Schuster, 1949.

Yardley, Jonathan. *Ring: An Biography of Ring Lardner.* New York: Random House, 1974.

Journal and Magazine Articles

Creamer, Robert W. "And Along Came Ruth." *Sports Illustrated,* 18 Mar. 1974, 74–90.

———. "Hit Opening in New York." *Sports Illustrated,* 25 Mar. 25 1974, 40–59.

Dashiell, Alfred S. "Football—The Overgrown Darling of the Press." *Independent,* 6 Nov. 1926, 520–21, 539.

Deford, Frank. "Hero with a Tragic Flaw." *Sports Illustrated,* 13 Jan. 1975, 51–58.

Gallico, Paul. "The Golden Decade." *Saturday Evening Post,* 5 Sept. 1931, 12–13, 113–15.

Jordan, Lester. "Sports Reporting Was a Scholarly Occupation Fifty Years Ago." *Editor and Publisher,* 2 July 1927, 9.

Niebuhr, Reinhold. "Heroes and Hero Worship." *Nation,* 23 Feb. 1921, 293.

Phinizy, Coles. "We Know of Knute, Yet Know Him Not." *Sports Illustrated,* 10 Sept. 1979, 98–112.

———. "Win One for the Gipper." *Sports Illustrated,* 17 Sept. 1979, 40–48.

Rice, Grantland. "Ace of Clubs." *Collier's,* 27 Sept. 1930, 15.

———. "Big Bill Tilden." *Collier's,* 29 Nov. 1924, 17, 45.

———. "Born to the Purple." *Collier's,* 12 Mar. 1927, 16.

———. "Boxing for a Million Dollars." *American Review of Reviews,* Oct. 1926, 416–20.

———. "Can Dempsey Come Back?" *Collier's,* 12 June 1926, 7.

———. "Collier's All-America Football Team." *Collier's,* 19 Dec. 1925, 6–8.

———. "Dempsey Couldn't Knock Him Down." *Collier's,* 31 Jan. 1925, 20.

———. "The French Wave." *Collier's,* 14 May 1927, 10.

———. "Have You Ever Seen Their Equals?" *Collier's,* 22 Nov. 22 1924, 12.

———. "How To Be a Champion." *Collier's,* 2 May 1925, 10.

———. "How Uncle Sam Has Created an Army of Athletes." *Scientific American,* 8 Feb. 1919, 114–15.

———. "If They Don't Think, They Lose." *Collier's*, 24 Jan. 1925, 17.

———. "Is Grange the Greatest?" *Collier's*, 20 Dec. 1924, 14, 38.

———. "My Greatest Thrill in Twenty-Two Years of Sport." *American Magazine*, May 1924, 41, 216–22.

———. "The Old Familiar Faces." *Collier's*, 2 Jan. 1926, 21.

———. "The Pigskin Ballyhoo." *Collier's*, 18 Sept. 1926, 20.

———. "The Return to Sport." *Country Life,* June 1919, 40–43.

———. "Rocks in the Glory Path." *Collier's,* 5 Mar. 1927, 28.

———. "The Sporting Thing." *Collier's*, 29 Aug. 1925, 12.

———. "The Stuff Men Are Made of." *Collier's*, 24 Oct. 1925, 27.

———. "Their Greatest Moments." *Collier's,* 16 May 1925, 20, 44.

———. "There's No Such Word as Quit." *Collier's*, 28 Feb. 1925, 13, 43.

———. "The Thrill of a Hard Fight." *Collier's,* 14 Nov. 1925, 14.

———. "To Beard the Lion." *Collier's*, 15 May 1926, 26.

———. "Too Much Money." *Collier's*, 12 Sept. 1925, 12.

———. "Under New Management." *Collier's,* 10 Oct. 1931, 23.

———. "Was Jack the Giant Killer?" *Collier's,* 28 May 1927, 9.

———. "What Draws the Crowds?" *Collier's*, 20 June 1925, 10, 44.

———. "Will Their Crowns Stay On?" *Collier's,* 27 Feb. 1926, 29.

———. "You Can't Win Without It." *Collier's*, 6 Dec. 1924, 16, 49.

Roberts, Randy. "Jack Dempsey: An American Hero in the 1920s." *Journal of Popular Culture* 8 (Fall 1974): 411–57, 426–72.

Smith, Red. "My Press-Box Memoirs." *Esquire*, Oct. 1975, 202–3, 250.

"Sports Dig Ever More Deeply into Newspapers' Editorial Space." *Editor and Publisher*, 28 Apr. 1928, 44.

Tunis, John R. "Gas and the Games." *Saturday Evening Post*, 25 Jan. 1930, 12–13, 44.

———. "The Newspapers and Sport." *Outlook and Independent*, 8 Jan. 1930, 68.

Underwood, John. "Was He the Greatest of All Time?" *Sports Illustrated*, 4 Sept. 1985, 114–31.

Newspaper Articles

Daley, Arthur. "Granny's Poetic Pen." *New York Times*, 21 Nov. 1954, 18(G).

———. "Sports of the Times." *New York Times*, 15 July 1954, 30.

Hawthorne, Fred. "Tilden Beaten; Three Frenchmen in Semi-Final." *New York Herald-Tribune*, 17 Sept. 1926, 1, 23.

"Mentor of Notre Dame's 'Four Horsemen' To Coach at Columbia." *New York Herald-Tribune*, 12 Dec. 1925, 1.

Rice, Grantland. "Bobby Jones Turns Back Evans' Brilliant Bid, Eliminating Chick, 3 and 2, in Title Golf." *New York Herald-Tribune*, 17 Sept. 1926, 23.

———. "Bobby Jones Wins National Amateur Golf Championship, 8 and 7." *New York Herald-Tribune*, 28 Aug. 1927, 1, 4(B).

———. "Dempsey Whips Sharkey by Seventh Round Knockout." *New York Herald-Tribune*, 22 July 1927, 1, 19.

———. "Engineers Ramble Over Vandy." *New York Herald-Tribune*, 11 Nov. 1928, 1(D).

———. "Grange Flashes Brilliantly in Final Contest." *New York Herald-Tribune*, 22 Nov. 1925, 3–4(J).

———. "Jack Dempsey Has Even Chance To Regain Crown, Rice Thinks." *New York Herald-Tribune*, 20 Sept. 1927, 29.

———. "Jones and Von Elm Reach Final for National Amateur Golf Crown by Decisive Victories." *New York Herald-Tribune*, 18 Sept. 1926, 14.

———. "More Athletic Activity and Interest Were Crowded into 1925 Than in any Previous Year." *New York Herald-Tribune*, 27 Dec. 1925, 4(J).

———. "Notre Dame Crushes Navy, 19 to 6, With Rally in the Second Half." *New York Herald-Tribune*, 16 Oct. 1927, 1–2(B).

———. "150,000 at Fight Tonight; Bettors Turn to Dempsey." *New York Herald-Tribune*, 22 Sept. 1927, 1, 27.

———. "Playing Short Pitches Correctly Made Bobby Jones Invincible." *New York Herald-Tribune*, 29 Aug. 1927, 12.

———. "Punch and Fighting Instinct Dempsey's Big Assets To-morrow." *New York Herald-Tribune*, 21 Sept. 1927, 25.

———. "Ruth Hits Three Home Runs as Yankees Win, 10-5." *New York Herald-Tribune*, 7 Oct. 1926, 1, 24.

———. "St. Louis Cardinals Win Series, Beat Yankees, 3-2." *New York Herald-Tribune*, 11 Oct. 1926, 1, 21.

———. "Shift in Betting and Questionable Defeat of Sharkey Raise Rumors Dempsey Had To Win." *New York Herald-Tribune*, 23 July 1927, 12.

———. "The Sportlight." *New York Herald-Tribune*, 14 Aug. 1925, 12; 29 Oct. 1925, 18; 6 Nov. 1925, 22; 27 Nov. 1925, 20; 5 Dec. 1925, 17; 12 Dec. 1925, 16; 15 Dec. 1925, 25; 17 Dec. 1925, 25; 18 Dec. 1925, 25; 25 Dec. 1925, 20; 29 Dec. 1925, 18; 2 Sept. 1926, 21; 23 Sept. 1926, 24; 25 Sept. 1926, 14; 29 Sept. 1926, 23; 13 Oct. 1926, 30; 19 Oct. 1926, 28; 26 July 1927, 19; 29 July 1927, 18; 10 Aug. 1927, 21; 12 Aug. 1927, 17; 27 Sept. 1927, 30; 29 Sept. 1927, 28; 6 Oct. 1927, 28; 8 Aug. 1928, 19; 21 Aug. 1928, 22.

———. "Tunney's Fighting Finish After Knock-Down in Seventh Round Proves Right to Title of Champion." *New York Herald-Tribune*, 24 Sept. 1927, 16.

———. "Tunney Wins From Dempsey; Keeps Title; 145,000 in Chicago Pay $3,000,000 To See Battle." *New York Herald-Tribune*, 23 Sept. 1927, 1, 25.

————. "Von Elm Wins Bobby Jones's Amateur Title." *New York Herald-Tribune*, 19 Sept. 1926, 1, 16.

————. "Weaving Grange-Like 82-Yard Run by Slagle Is Highlight of Tigers' Decisive Triumph." *New York Herald-Tribune*, 15 Nov. 1925, 3(J).

————. "Yale Proves It Has One of the Country's Great Teams in Day of Startling Football Results." *New York Herald-Tribune*, 2 Nov. 1925, 18.

————. "Yankees Win from Pirates Again, 6-2, as Pipgras Stars." *New York Herald-Tribune*, 7 Oct. 1927, 1, 25.

————. "Yankees Win Third in Row as Pennock Stills Pirates, 8 to 1." *New York Herald-Tribune*, 8 Oct. 1927, 1, 17.

"Ruth Keeps Air Mail Promise of Homer for Boy Near Death." *New York Herald-Tribune*, 7 Oct. 1926, 1.

"738,555 Gridiron Fans Have Paid To See Grange." *New York Herald-Tribune*, 25 Nov. 1925, 20.

"70,000 See Grange Win, 19-7." *New York Herald-Tribune*, 7 Dec. 1925, 1.

"Want Grange in Congress." *New York Times*, 11 Nov. 1925, 20.

Thesis

Kilborn, Robert. "Sports Journalism in the 1920s: A Study of the Interdependence of the Daily Newspaper and the Sports Hero." Master's thesis, Michigan State University, 1972.

Index